URBANISATION, STREET CHILDREN AND THEIR PROBLEMS

URBANISATION, STREET CHILDREN AND THEIR PROBLEMS

By

N.K. Behura

&

R.P. Mohanty

Nabakrushna Choudhury Centre for Development Studies, Orissa Bhubaneswar–751 013

D P H

DISCOVERY PUBLISHING HOUSE

NEW DELHI-110002

First Published-2005

ISBN 81-7141-924-0

Published by
DISCOVERY PUBLISHING HOUSE
4831/24, Ansari Road, Prahlad Street,
Darya Ganj, New Delhi-110002 (India)
Phone: 23279245 • Fax: 91-11-23253475
E-mail:dphtemp@indiatimes.com

Printed at:
Amit Enterprises, Delhi

Foreword

The world civilisation is moving spirally with the advancement in the fields of science and technology. Developed nations have made wonderful achievement in various fields and spheres. Having made some provisions for the basic needs of their population, they have made an attempt to conquer the outer space and are on the brink of conquering other planets.

Following the footprints of advancement nations, developing nations have been striving to accelerate the process of their development so as to meet the basic requirements of people.

But they have not succeeded in their effort due to growing population, unbalanced development and deprivation of a large number of people belonging to the backward classes of the society. Even though the rate of growth of income has touched 6 per cent or so per year during the last decade, it has not solved the problem of unemployment, poverty, inequality and destitution because of abysmal poverty. Due to unemployment, many parents do not bother to take care of their children.

In fact, millions of children in India are deprived of their childhood rights, Article 46 of the Constitution envisages that children upto the age of 14 be provided with free and compulsory primary education. But this has not been realised till now, besides other deprivations, which have made their life miserable. Fast growing population on the one hand and acute poverty on the other has pushed millions of poor children into the streets of all the growing cities and towns. Street children are mostly concentrated in urban and industrial areas. Such children living in urban slums and streets are exploited in manifold ways. They are totally deprived of their childhood rights.

Many of the international organisations, like UNICEF, UN, WHO, CARE, UNDP, etc. have been assisting child-development programmes. In spite of their generous help, not much has been achieved in this front. Welfare and development of street children must be the concern of every well-to-do citizen of the country. If these children are allowed to lead a vicious life, the future of the country will be jeopardized. Children are the future citizens of the country and prosperity of the nation has a stake in their welfare and development.

The present study provides some insight into the magnitude of this problem in Bhubaneswar, the capital city of Orissa. NKC Centre for Development Studies has been undertaking such crucial studies in the context of national interest. I thank Prof. N.K. Behura, Honorary Fellow and Dr. Ramesh Prasad Mohanty, for their strenuous effort in making such a worthwhile study.

I hope that this book will be very useful for the researchers, academicians, administrators, NGO activists, students of Social Work, Social Anthropology and all those who are interested in the problems of the children in general and street children in particular.

Prof. B. Misra
Former Director and Chairman
and at present Research Advisor,
N.K.C. Centre for Development Studies,
Orissa

Preface

Indian population is growing very fast due to the persistence of illiteracy, ignorance and traditional believes amongst a major chunk of the populace. It was about 36 crore (361088090) in 1951. But during the lapse of last four decades, it has increased to about 85 crore (846302688) in 1991 thereby indicating more than 134 per cent growth. With this large population, India, now ranks as the second most populous country of the world, and at it was apprehended, by the end of 2000 A.D., it has crossed 100 crore mark. If this pace of population growth continues, it would cross the population of China and become the most populous country of the world if no concerted effort is made immediately both at the macro as well as micro levels. It would exert a lot of pressure on the available resources and create insurmountable new socio-economic problems, and aggravate the problem of flourishing immigration of rural wage-earning people to urban centres.

Educationally the people of India are very backward (literacy is only 52.21 per cent as per 1991 census. It was merely 16.10 per cent in 1951 and a majority are basically rural based. They are also very religious minded. Most of them think that the children born to them are the gift of God and since God has created them, it has also arranged a natural mechanism to feed them. Hence, these people conceptualise that when they will be able to move on their limbs, they will earn for themselves and also for their parents. Hence, the rural people consider that unnecessary intervention in family planning at the individual level is nothing but a sin against the desire of the almighty. It would create disaster for the well-being of the family if something negative is done to shatter the ideology. Through the ages, this age-old belief has been significantly contributing to rapid growth of Indian population and has thus created an imbalance between the available resources and the growing population.

In the recent past India has celebrated 50 years of her independence but she has not yet been able to check her population growth or develop sufficient human resources for eco-friendly management and utilisation of resources. In rural areas, where the growth of population is faster than urban areas, the people have considerably exploited the existing resources and no more gainful work is available for them to earn their daily bread. As a result, the people in difficult situations rush to their accessible urban centres in order to each and stay alive. These people result in creation and development of slums in urban centres. But because of restricted urban resources and limited revenue of the government, all of them do not get even minimum civic amenities or 'Urban Basic Services' (UBC). In such situations, they are forced to lead wretched living and fail to feed their children properly and also educate them, either partly because of their helpless poor economic condition or because of unavailability of institutional facility within or around their residential zones. Under such pressing situations parents ask their children to work for their own survival and also for the family. These children come forward to work on streets as rag-pickers, shoe-shiners, hotel workers, garbage workers, domestic servants, vendors, hawkers etc. They work very hard throughout the day from early morning to evening and even in some cases till late night depending upon the call of their families. If a child does not work according to the demand of his/her parents he/she is often scolded, beaten up or even given less or no food. Thus, they lead a pitiable life.

The Directive Principle of State Policy of our constitution advocates that 'the state shall, in particular, direct its policy towards securing that children are given opportunities and facilities to develop in a healthy manner and in conditions of freedom and dignity and their childhood and youth are protected against exploitation and against moral and material abandonment'. In order to give a fruitful shape to this policy, over the years, various legislations and policies have been enacted. Some of these are National Health Policy-1982, Juvenile Justice Act-1986, National

Policy on Nutrition-1993 etc. Apart from these, as per, the Article-2 of the United Nations Convention on 'Right of the Child', each child irrespective of caste, creed, age and sex has the right to have sufficient nutrition, medical care, education, housing, recreation etc. But practically these are hard enough to reach at each child working on streets.

Today there are about 71 million children living in urban centres of which *18 million live in urban slums* and surprisingly the number of children working on streets of different cities of India *together constitute the largest in the world* (cf. Panicker, 1993: 6). But very unfortunately these children do not get even the minimum requirements and amenities, like clothing, nutrition, education, medical care, security, recreational facilities etc.

In the recent past, UNICEF in collaboration with the Ministry of Welfare, Government of India, has conducted some specific studies on 'Situational Analysis of Street Children in 14 different cities of India and finds that most of the children are working in informal sectors and earn meager income to suffice their hunger but as many of them do not even earn a hand to mouth income, they starve.

In accordance with the above perspectives, i.e. the present study, an attempt has been made to focus about the socio-economic condition of the street children in Bhubaneswar city. It also explains the family background of these children, that is, under which circumstances they have come to work on streets, their day-to-day problems and how do they struggle for their survival. The whole problem and findings have been dealt with 7 chapters. The first two chapters speak about the methodological backdrop and the process and development of urban features of Bhubaneswar city which attracted a huge mass of rural wage—earning people from within and adjoining states. The next three chapters deal with family milieu, social-economic profile of the street children, their problems and struggle for existence. The sixth chapter deals with some of the legislative and welfare measures and also puts forth some other development measures for the benefit and welfare of these children at the wider perspective.

We express our earnest gratitude to Prof. Dr. B. Misra, the former Chairman, NCDS, for according permission and encouraging us to carry out this research project. We are grateful to Prof. Dr. G.C. Kar, Director, NCDS, for all the help he has extended to complete this piece of research from the beginning to the end.

We hope that this work will be very useful to the development administrators, academicians, researchers, social scientists and NGO activists who are engaged and are interested in the welfare and development of the street children.

N.K. Behura

R.P. Mohanty

Contents

1

Introduction

Street children comprise a major social problem in India from various viewpoints. It is a despicable problem not only in the developing countries but also in some of the developed countries also. The problem is more seriously in industrialised and urbanised countries of the world. However, rapid emergence of the street children in developing cities of any country is considered as a natural phenomenon all over the world as the poorest of the poor masses of the rural areas migrate to their accessible cities under the operating forces of 'push and pull' factors. They comprehensively hope of getting regular employment in cities and thereby leading a better living over there. Such poor and hapless people settle down in slums, pavements, railway platforms, but stations, abandoned construction sites etc. and also in some cases in the backyards of some city residents. Their over accumulation in these places, however, gradually aggrandize the problem.

At the initial stage the poor immigrants find it very troublesome to adjust and earn their daily bread in the new environment and ecological setting and in due course of time they become individualistic in nature because of a number of entangled factors, like large family size coupled with appalling poverty and lack of easy and quick approach to earn sufficiently for the whole family. In such a situation the household head and other adults take to any occupation, no matter, whether it is a socially low or economically un-lucrative. Normally they take to occupations, like rickshaw pulling, wage-earning, vending, doing petty business, working as unskilled or semi-skilled construction workers and ask their children to take up earning activities that do not require any capital for investment, like rag-picking, begging, cleaning of train coaches and passenger buses etc. Some parents however, engage their children in vending of tea, egg, snacks etc. and shoe-polishing at railway platforms and bus stations etc., and some other compel their children to work as domestic aids and maid servants, doing sundry works in hotels and garages etc. and earn daily for their self as well as for other members of their families.

Fathers are often cruel towards their sons, but mothers are relatively sympathetic. Fathers are harsh because the whole responsibility of feeding all the family members lies on them and when they find difficulties to meet the demand they resort to regular alcoholic drinks and spend a major portion of their income on it. As a result, in many cases, they compel their school going children to earn and contribute to the family's income. Sometimes they fix up some target amount of money to be earned by their children daily and sometimes, when a child fails to earn the targeted amount or when he throws himself into the playground instead of working, he is scolded, beaten up and even the quantity of his food is either reduced or his meal is denied for the day. It creates a desperate and harassing shock in the mind of the child and one day he runs away from home and comes on to the street to lead his life independently. He takes of any work he likes, eats anything he gets, and sleeps anywhere he finds suitable; it may be a railway platform, incomplete or abandoned building, pavement, market, bus station, or even the open sky. In course of time he forgets his family, neglects his personal hygienic care and constantly struggles for his survival. At times he is economically exploited and physically abused by the public and, under such conditions he suffers from deep emotional shocks.

Because of the gender disability, conservative Indian culture and societal norms of division of labour, the girls cannot take to any outside vulnerable activities. A minor girl child is asked to work on the streets along with her elders for collecting rags or vending fruits or doing any other such activity. But when she becomes a major, her parents prefer to engage her in less hazardous and more secured and gender specific earning activities; most preferable being sundry domestic service. In this type of work, she cleans utensils, clothes, house floor, and also in some cases tends children of the employing households. She receives a meager monthly remuneration in addition to some annual incentives like, new or old clothing, dress materials, occasional foodstuffs or food that may be fresh or stale or leftover of the previous night. At times she also receives some cash incentives during festive occasions.

The daily or occasional food-incentives she collects from her employing households are accumulated everyday by her and shared among the family members or only among the children. But what is actually more pitiable is that unfortunately, if the girl has some brothers, her share of her own collection of food comes to be minimal because of the gender biasness in patriarchal Indian societies. Thus, the girl children of these people are hard-pressed and are under nourished. This situation creates frustrating experience among them. In some cases, they decide to leave home permanently but ultimately they fall prey to the antisocial public in streets. They are sexually abused, economically exploited and physically harassed. Thus, the situation of slum children in general and street children in particular is more vulnerable compared to their counterparts living in organised rural and urban housing settlements. Most of them lack of education, immunisation, sanitation, destitution and thus lead life of uncertainly and insecurity.

Street Children; Their Identity

The street children are known after various terms in different countries of the world. In northern developed countries they are known as *homeless-youth, runaways* or even *throwaways*. In developing countries, like Kenya, they are called as *parking boys*, in the Philippines they are known as *pogey-boys*, in Brazil they are called as *'pivets'* and in India they are normally known as *'rag-pickers'*. Interestingly, in Peru they are popularly known as *'pajaro-frutero'* meaning fruit bird, in Colombia, *gamin* meaning kid having negative connotation. In Zaire, these children are called as *'moineaox'* meaning sparrows and in Cameroon, *'poussins'*, meaning chicks (Pandey, 1991: 15-16).

There are controversies and technical difficulties in defining street children for unanimous acceptance all over the world as the situational aspects of these children differ from country to country and even place to place within a country. However, UNICEF (1988) defines street children as, "...those for whom the street (in the widest sense of the word; i.e., unoccupied dwellings, wasteland, etc..), is more than their family, has become their real home, a situation in which there is no protection, supervision or direction from responsible adults".

The define the street children, United Kingdom Committee (1980) for UNICEF gives stress on the basis of their relationship with their families. It advocates that not all the street children are alike and observes that:

(i) About 75 per cent of street children maintain contact with families. They work on the street either under the supervision of employers inside or outside their family or are in business for themselves. They spend most nights with their family, contrary to popular belief.

(ii) A growing percentage, currently some 20 per cent, spend all their days and some nights on the streets or in public places. Their families have not abandoned them, nor they have abandoned their families, but poverty, violence, drink and sexual abuse have forced them out of their homes. These children are increasingly vulnerable to the abuse and exploitation of street life and often develop a very negative view of themselves; and

(iii) Children who have no family at all make up 5 per cent of all street children. They include orphans, runaways, refugees; these abandoned children suffer from deep emotional disturbance".

On the basis of the above observations, the said committee for UNICEF categorises the street children into three broad groups for the purpose of better understanding and for facilitating the implementation of welfare programmes. These three groups are:

(A) The Children on the Street

These children have more or less continuous family contacts. Their focus in life is still their home. A very few children of this category attend school and also work. Most of them return home at the end of each working day and have a sense of belonging to the local community in which their home is situated.

(B) Children of the Street

This group of street children is smaller and more complex in nature. The children of this group consider street as their home where they seek shelter, food and a sense of family among companions. Family ties exist for them but they have occasional and infrequent contact with their families.

(C) Abandoned Children

This group may appear to form a part of the second group. However, by virtue of having severed all ties with a biological family, they are entirely on their own, not just for material but also for psychological survival.

In a background paper on street children, submitted at the National workshop on street children held in New Delhi (1988), UNICEF also clarifies that the appellation 'street children' is one which often highlights a certain set of working and living conditions rather than personal or social characteristics of the individual children themselves. Too often, children in these conditions are victims of stereotypes such as 'juvenile delinquents' for the public and authorities. It further says that the term 'street children' should refer to "all children who work in the streets of urban areas without reference to the time they spend there or the reasons for being there".

Indian Situation

In India, the street children have been categorised into three groups based on the relationships and contact with their families. These three groups are as follows:

(i) Children who live with their families, whether it be on the street, in slums, or wasteland or abandoned/ derelict building, etc. but spend a lot of time working or hanging about on the street; it has been estimated that this group is the largest of the three categories.

(ii) Children who live and work on the street (i.e. in the widest sense of the word), yet maintain occasional contacts with their families who live either in other cities or, more often, in rural areas. These children, sometimes, send money to their near kins. They see the street as their home.

(iii) Children who live and work on the street (i.e. in the widest sense of the word) have no family contacts whatsoever. These children are neither orphan nor abandoned or neglected by or estranged from their families (Reddy, 1992: 2-3).

For the purpose of implementing action plans for the welfare and betterment of the street children in India, Ministry of Welfare, Government of India, indicates that the "street children" should mean and include the following:

(i) Children who live on the streets or pavements;

(ii) Children who live in slums but spend most of their time on the streets and are engaged in various activities; and

(iii) Children who work in:

  (a) Street trades, such as, rag-picking, petty business, vending and shoe-shining;

  (b) Manual jobs as collies, helpers, cleaners, rickshaw pullers etc.; and

  (c) Employment in wayside tea-stalls, restaurants, automobile garages, tyre and tube workshops, machine shops etc. (1990:1).

The above diversified and overlapping definitions inherit some difficulties for accepting any one definition unanimously. As a result, various attempts have been made from different angles including careful canvas of sociological literatures to itemize the following identifying traits of street children in India. (Pandey, 1991:19). These traits are as follows:

(i) *Place of Residence:* Place of congregation is street, unoccupied dwellings, waste lands, public places etc.

(ii) *A Set of Working Conditions:* Street is the work-place, the work they do is of very low status and it bears bad taste, and the return is paltry.

(iii) *A Set of Living Conditions:* They live most of their life in the street as if their real home.

(iv) *Time Spent on the Street:* They spend all their days and nights or some nights on the street or in the public places.

(v) *Protection, Supervision and Direction:* There is lack of or inadequate, protection, supervision and direction, they fend for themselves.

(vi) *Family Relationship:* There may be street children with continuous family contact, occasional family contact, and without family contact.

(vii) *Vulnerability:* They are vulnerable to ills of urbanisation (ibid: pp. 19-20).

To these identifying traits of street children. Mohsin adds five more attributes which could be useful in identifying the parameters for future studies related to the problems of street children in the third world countries. These five attributes are:

(i) *Social Status:* The street children are looked down upon with condemnation.

(ii) *Perception about Self:* Completely lacking.

(iii) *Educational Status:* They are illiterate (barring a few).

(iv) *Application of Life's Meaningful Activities:* Moderate

(v) *Value Orientation:* They are largely individualistic (1994: 16).

What more can be added to these attributes is that the street children are very reluctant to interact with the public because of their fear, low social status suspicion and feeling of being a separate entity of the society.

Objectives of the Study

The broad objectives of the present study are four-fold. These are:

(a) to analyse the situational aspects of the street children in Bhubaneswar city;

(b) to find out the factors responsible for their distressing socio-economic as well as socio-psychological conditions;

(c) to find out educational choices and their aspirational levels; and

(d) to suggest some remedial measures for the welfare of these children.

The Universe and Methodology

Taking into consideration the time constraint, scope and limitation of the present study, a total number of 120 street children (below 14 years of age) of Bhubaneswar city residing in 8 different pockets/areas within the municipal boundary were selected on the basis of simple random sampling procedure.

At the first state, the pockets namely: (1) Rajmahal/Market-building/Kalpana, (2) Railway station/Cuttack road, (3) FCI Malgodown/Sriya talkies, (4) Saheed Nagar/Satyanagar, (5) Chandrasekharpur/Sikhar Chandi, (6) Jayadev Vihar/Salia Sahi, (7) Baramunda/CRPF area and (8) Ainginia/Dumuduma were selected purposively where street children are concentrated. From each pocket of the area, a total number of 15 samples were selected on the basis of simple random sampling giving weightage to cover at least 25 per cent of girl street children of the total sample. A detail profile of the sample taken from different pockets is furnished in Table—1.1.

Data Collection and Tools of Research

The study has made use of various anthropological methods, like collection of primary data through structured schedule (Appendix: 1), observation, interview, case studies etc. The study has also made use of secondary data collected from various sources, like census documents, municipal documents, different libraries in the city and local NGO sectors working on the streets children. Apart from this, we have also taken the help of street educators of the Orissa State Council for Child Welfare (OSCCW) in organising the street children at different pockets of the city.

Scope and Limitation of the Study

The sample size of the study is small. But the scope of the study is very broad since this is an in-depth study. Each of the 120 sample has been personally interviewed by the authors with a view to have reliable data on which concrete conclusions could be made. The study would be very useful to the academicians, civil societies, students, researchers, government officials and all those who are interested in the problems of street children.

Literature Survey

A number of studies have been made on the street children by various individual researchers, academicians, research institutions and NGO activists in India and abroad. But in Orissa, the number of studies made on this area of problem is very limited.

A workshop on *"street children and slum children: legal protection and social security"* was organised by socio-legal aid research and training centre, Calcutta, in collaboration with the institute of urban management, and Calcutta Municipal Corporation on 6th November, 1988. It was a follow-up workshop of the National Seminar on *"Child Abuse and Neglect: Prevention and Protection of Working Children, Abandoned and Neglected children"* held in Calcutta in 1988. The report of the workshop came out in 1990 in a volume edited by Mandal. The report explains a number of protective measures such as national policy for children, declaration of the rights of child, ILO perspective on child labour, juvenile justice Act-1986 and the child labour protection and regulation act 1986 etc.

Apart from this the workshop also looked into various issues on social security and legal protection of the ill-fated children including the basic needs of the street children and slum children, need of nutritional programme, health and sanitary requirements, educational facilities available and the need of vocational training, recreational facilities, possibility of coverage of the street children in the Integrated Child Development Scheme (ICDS) etc.

Pandey (1991) has conducted a study entitled 'Situational Analysis of Street Children' in Kanpur city. The project was sponsored by Ministry of Welfare, Government of India and UNICEF.

He has taken 1250 sample of street children in few wards of the above city and has examined the nature and extent of the problems of the street children and the familial milieu they are enmeshed in. He has also assessed their basic needs, deprivation, located the existing services and has also made some policy recommendations and research suggestions.

In his study he finds that:

(a) A large majority of sample belong to boy street children (82.7%) and rest (17.3%) are girl street children.

(b) About 90 per cent (89.8) of street children work on the street and return to home at the end of the day's work.

(c) The second largest category comprises the runaways; the children who have left home and are living on the street. These children constitute 6.5 per cent of the total sample.

(d) The smallest category of street children is made up of push-outs or throwaway children who comprise merely 3.7 per cent. These children do not have any home to return.

(e) As regards the factors responsible for making the children to come up to the street for work, 67.3 per cent are because of their poverty, followed by 12.1 per cent who have come on to the streets due to untimely death of their parents and 11.1 per cent have come in search of employment by self. He has also attributed some other factors, like strained parent-child relationship, broken-home, pull of the city etc.

(f) About 98 per cent of street children do not have any opportunity for sports and games.

(g) Nearly 81 per cent have aspirations, desires and wishes in their mind.

(h) Slightly more than 38 per cent aspire for regular service, 22.7 per cent for education, 14.7 per cent for business, 5 per cent for vocational training and very few (0.6%) for marriage.

(i) A substantial chunk, i.e. 53.6 per cent have friends, relatives and peers in the locality.

(j) In majority of cases the family size comes to 7 to 9 members.

(k) In case of 77.3 per cent, both the parents are alive.

(l) The age of father mainly falls in the group of 41-50.

(m) Majority of children (81.6%) express their view that their needs are met by their parents.

(n) In case of 95.6 per cent cases the parent-child relationship seems to be very cordial.

Arimpoor (1992) has studied the street children in Madras city under a sponsored project. He has found out the nature and gravity of the problem of the street children in the said city. Like Pandey (1991), he has also meticulously highlighted the physical, psychological, and social problems and their requirements. Further he has suggested modifications of existing services and programmes for the betterment of these children. The salient features of his findings are as follows:

(a) that of the total sample, 22 per cent work as coolie, 10.4 per cent work as hotel workers, 8 per cent work as rickshaw-pullers, 9.6 per cent work as rag-pickers, 7.1 per cent work as flower sellers. Others include automobile cleaners and helpers, small scale industry employees, vendors, construction workers etc.

(b) Majority of them work for 10-12 hours per day.

(c) As many as 90 per cent of children live with their parents and very few are found to be orphans.

(d) About 88 per cent fathers as against only 39.9 per cent mothers of the street children are employed.

(e) Majority of them (82.8%) are from Chennai (Madras) city itself and the rest have migrated from other places of Tamil Nadu and some other states.

(f) About 68 per cent of children claim that they are undernourished.

(g) So far as the health is concered, 18.5 per cent have good health and 68.5 per cent are moderately healthy.

(h) These children are not allowed to enter into the public and private parks because of their unkempt appearance; they play during sick-hours.

(i) About 70 per cent of them say that they need education and 48.2 per cent opine that it would be better if facility for employment is created for them.

(j) Nearly 62 per cent have adequate clothing followed by 38 per cent who have inadequate clothing and 74 per cent do not have any winter garments.

(k) The ambition of the children include teachership, acquiring the skill of tailoring, becoming mechanic, undertaking business, becoming vehicle drivers etc.

Like the above, a similar study has also been conducted in Bangalore city by Reddy (1992). She finds that:

(a) About 80, 16, 4 and 0.11 per cent of sample street children are Hindu, Muslim, Christian and others respectively.

(b) Nearly 23, 6 and 71 per cent belong to Scheduled Caste, Scheduled Tribe and general communities respectively.

(c) In case of 21.66 per cent, the fathers of street children are not alive, and in case of 8.74 per cent their mothers are dead.

(d) In most of the cases, the age of fathers fail in the age grade of 41-50 years.

(e) About 18 per cent of children are aggressive and 81.26 are submissive.

(f) Nearly 85 per cent have some type of ambition and 15.31 per cent do not have any ambition in life.

(g) In case of 89.92 per cent, the fathers are employed.

(h) Most of the parents work as coolie (26.69%) followed by 19.5 per cent who work as Vendor and 12.51 per cent as labourer.

(i) The reasons of living in street is mainly because of poverty (73.98%), desertion/death of parents (18.71%) unemployment (59.06%) etc.

(j) About 99 per cent of children are exposed to smoke, dirt and filth.

(k) Little more than 80 per cent of street children have night shelter with covered roofs and 19.60 per cent stay on the street.

(l) About 87 per cent of children are undernourished and 7.89 per cent are severely undernourished.

(m) About 84 per cent children possess moderate health and 13.71 per cent have bad health. Good health is observed only in case of 1.77 per cent of them.

In 1992 a state level workshop on the "*programme strategies for children especially in difficult circumstances*" was organised in Bhubaneswar city. The workshop report provides some useful background materials on these children and the action taken by the social welfare ministry, urban local bodies, Non Governmental Organisations (NGOs) etc.

In 1994, a state level workshop on "*Government and NGO participation for street children and working children*" was jointly organised by the state council for child welfare and UNICEF, Bhubaneswar. The workshop focused some majority issues like the factors responsible for the emergence of street children, how do they struggle for their survival and growth, their major problems etc.

A study conducted in Indore city by Phillips (1991) also reveals the same interesting characteristics. He has studied 300 street children below the age of 16 years from different patches of the city to know about the living conditions of these children and has analysed the physical, psychological, economic factors and the social conditions in which the street children are living. He has also attempted to highlight the existing services reaching them through Government and NGO sectors.

His findings speak that about 36 per cent of his sample do not belong to the Indore city itself, 12 per cent of children have no information about their family, 25.3 per cent do not live with their parents, and 40 per cent of them lack permanent place to reside.

He has categorised that 70.7 per cent of the total sample belong to the category of '*children on the street*', 19 per cent '*of the street*' and rest 10.3 per cent are '*abandoned children*'. The other important findings are that: (1) 86.3 and 13.7 per cent are boys and girls respectively, (2) maximum number of children fall in the age group of 12-14 (29.0%) and 10-12 (26.0%), (3) 65 per cent the illiterate, (4) the average family size is 5.4 and the average per household income comes to Rs. 910.1, (5) of the total 1379 family members of the street children studied, 41.3 per cent are unemployed, (6) about 83 per cent of the street children have 2-4 friends and 17 per cent do not have any friends, (7) children in the age group of 10-12 and 12-14 are mainly engaged in working at tea stalls, garages and in hotels, (8) nearly 54 per cent children are satisfied with their jobs and the rest 45.3 per cent are not, (9) the tea stall and hotel boys work for about 12 to 14 hours a day, (10) on an average, the rag pickers get Rs. 8/- to 12/- per day; the shoe-shiners earn about Rs. 10/- to 11/-, the beggars earn about Rs. 7/-, the tea stall boys Rs. 9/-

and the garage boys Rs. 8/- per day, and (11) these children generally suffer from T.B., measles, fever, and blisters and wounds.

Table 1.1: Area and sample of street children

Sl. No.	*Pockets/Area*	*Boys*	*Girls*	*Total*
1.	Rajmahal/Market-building/Kalpana	13 (10.83)	2 (1.67)	15 (12.5)
2.	Railway Station/ Cuttack Road	11 (9.17)	4 (3.33)	15 (12.5)
3.	FCI Malgodam/ Sriya Talkies	11 (9.17)	4 (3.33)	15 (12.5)
4.	Saheed Nagar/ Satya Nagar	7 (5.83)	8 (6.62)	15 (12.5)
5.	Chandrasekharpur/ Sikharchandi	12 (10.0)	3 (2.5)	15 (12.5)
6.	Jayadev Vihar Salia Sahi	12 (10.0)	3 (2.5)	15 (12.5)
7.	Baramunda/CRP	11 (9.17)	4 (3.33)	15 (12.5)
8.	Ainginia/Dumuduma	13 (10.83)	2 (1.67)	15 (12.5)
	Total	**90 (75.0)**	**30 (25.0)**	**120 (100.0)**

Note: Figures in brackets represent %age to the total sample.

2

Profile of Bhubaneswar City

Location and Communication

Bhubaneswar is the new capital of the state of Orissa and a growing city in eastern India. It is located between 20°-12′ - 42″ and 20°-18′ -47″ N latitudes and 85° -47′ -18″ to 85°-53′ -0″ E longitudes and it comes at a height of about 140 feet above the 'Mean Sea Level' (cf. B.M.C, 1995: 2). The city is found almost at the middle portion of the state on its eastern side and it falls in the district of Khurdha.

The city runs from North-East to South-West along the coastal plains belt (cf. G.O.1, 1971: 1). It comes under South-Eastern railway service facility at a distance of about 435 km away from Kolkata in the east and 1215 km from Chennai in the south by the shortest railway route.

Cuttack, a class-I city of Orissa is only 29 kilometers away from Bhubaneswar city at its southern side. Recently these two cities have been linked together through development of four-way road links with the financial assistance from the World Bank. It is going to be the first twin-city of the state almost coinciding with the planning of south Indian twin-city, the Hyderabad-Secunderabad.

The city is well connected with various important roadways including the National Highway No. 5 and it is also linked with different metropolis of the country through various airways, particularly Indian Airlines.

So far as the nomenclature of Bhubaneswar city is concerned, it is otherwise popularly known as the *'Temple City'* of India. It is also known as the *Kalinga Nagari* (City of Kalinga), *Tribhubaneswar.* (The seat of the lord of the Universe), *Ekamra Kshetra* (Mango orchard), *Siva Pitha* (Shrine of lord Siva) etc. Finally the name of the place became *Bhubaneswar*, after the name of the Lord Lingaraj who is otherwise known as Bhubaneswar meaning the lord of *Bhuban* or earth (cf. Times Communication, 1994: 1).

Historical Background and Present Administrative Status

Since ancient times, Bhubaneswar has been a very important place because of its rich religious and socio-cultural heritage, environmental, geographical and geological significance. As a result of this, it was an important sacred and administrative centre during the reign of various emperors and kings of ancient and medieval arise.

From the rock inscriptions available in a number of archaeological sites and remains in and around Bhubaneswar city, its history is traced back from the 1st century or even before that.

During the remote past, Arise was forming a part of ancient kingdom of Kalinga. The Nandas of Magadha dynasty were the first to rule Kalinga. After the downfall of the Nanda dynasty it became independent but the emperor Ashoka of Mourya dynasty invaded Kalinga around 261 B.C. and ultimately conquered it after the great bloody Kalinga war occurred at Dhauligiri, a hill site at the periphery of the modern Bhubaneswar city. The sad incidents of the war are edicted in the rock walls of Dhauligiri sites (3rd century B.C.) which still exist there for remembering the event.

During the 1st century B.C. the king Kharabela of Chedi dynasty reigned Kalinga. A rock inscription on the Udaygiri hills of Bhubaneswar city, records his life and 13 years of his administration.

After 1st century B.C., Kalinga came under the administration of the Satavahan upto 202 A.D. Then emperor

Samudragupta of Gupta dynasty invaded Kalinga around 350 A.D. and the Matharas ruled it upto 498 A.D. Following the Matharas, the Eastern Gangas occupied Kalinga. After the Gangas, the sailodbhavas ruled over Kongoda Mandala comprising the districts of Ganjam and Puri including Bhubaneswar. They acknowledged the king Sasanka as their overlord till 619 A.D. The Somavamsis who were known as Kesharis established their dynasty in Kalinga about in middle of 7th century A.D. In this context, the genealogy of the dynasty is available in Brahmeswar temple inscriptions of Bhubaneswar. During the reign of Uddyot Keshary (840-880 A.D.) many temples were constructed in and round Bhubaneswar city and it became an important pilgrim spot. The world famous Lingaraj temple of Bhubaneswar also took its birth during Keshary dynasty.

The imperial Gangas succeeded the Kesharies and ruled Kalinga till 1435 A.D. with Kalinganagar (ancient name of Bhubaneswar) as its capital.

During the reign of several emperors of this era and also of the solar dynasty, hundreds of temples again took birth with very high artistic and architectural significance throughout the eastern Arise including Bhubaneswar. Later on the King Mukunda Dev of the Bhoi dynasty, being the last Hindu ruler of Kalinga also gave much importance on the development of religious architectures in the city. Unfortunately after him, when the Afghan rule started in 1568 A.D. in Arise, all the temples and archaeological creations were destroyed by them. Most of the temples in and around Bhubaneswar city were completely disfigured and also dismantled and most of them were lost in the dark. Arise came under the Mughal rule in 1575 A.D. and Maratha rule in Arise succeeded the Mughals in 1751 A.D. The Maratha encouraged pilgrimage in Arise, (cf. G.O.I, 1988: 1-2; G.O.D, 1990: 183-283; Times Communication, 1994: A-1 and Mohanty, 1998, 25-27).

On 17th December, 1803 A.D. the Maratha rule ended and the British administration came into being in Arise. The British rule continued till 1947. (cf. G.O.O. 1990: 219).

Before 1912, Arise was a division of Bengal presidency. During that time, it was comprising 4 districts, viz. Cuttack, Puri, Balasore and Angul-cum-Khondmals. Apart from this, it has 17 feudatory states within its jurisdiction. In the year of 1905 Sambalpur district was added including 2 feudatory states of Chota Nagpur, viz., Gangpur and Bonai and 5 feudatory states from central provinces, viz. Patna, Kalahandi, Sonpur, Bamra and Rairakhol. Thus, by the end of 1911 the Arise division had 5 districts and 24 feudatory states. Immediately thereafter, i.e. in 1912 the Bihar and Arise province was formed after the separation of their jurisdiction from the Bengal presidency. The composite province of Arise and Bihar continued till 31st March 1936 and on 1st April, 1936 Arise became a separate province under the Government of India Act of 1935 (cf. G.O.I: 1991: 17-18 and Mohanty, 1998: 27-68) with Cuttack as its capital. But because of a number of prospective physical and other socio-economic features of Bhubaneswar, during the second Congress ministry, on 30th September, 1946, a motion was brought in the Legislative Assembly to shift the capital from Cuttack to Bhubaneswar. The resolution was passed unanimously and during the chiefministership of Dr. Harekrushna Mahatab, Pandit Jawaharlal Nehru, the then Prime Minister of India, laid the foundation of the new capital of Arise at Bhubaneswar on 13 April 1948. The construction of building for various offices progressed in full swing and the Arise Legislative Assembly was shifted from Cuttack to Bhubaneswar in 1949 (cf. G.O.I; 1970: 240).

Development of Civic Administration Status

Bhubaneswar was a small sacred town in 1921 because of its religious importance. Later on it became a class IV town and retained the same status until 1951. But in 1961 it was recognised as a class III town and finally in 1971, it became class I depending on its population strength and other urban characteristics (cf. G.O.I. 1971: 5).

As per the Municipal Act (Bihar-Arise) 1922, Bhubaneswar came under the administration of notified area committee on 1st February, 1948. With a total population of 16,512 during 1951 census, in 1952 it was administered under Notified Area Council (N.C.C.) with effect from 1st October, 1952 to 11th March, 1979 (As per Arise Municipal Act, 1950) and then on 12th March, 1979 Bhubaneswar Municipality was established. The town enjoyed this status until 14th August, 1994. The day after, on 15th August, 1994, Bhubaneswar was declared as a corporation and Bhubaneswar Municipal Corporation (B.M.C.) was constituted to succeed its prior status (cf. B.M.C. 1995: 4).

Development of Urban Features

After the establishment of the state capital in Bhubaneswar, many private residential colonies, namely Bapuji Nagar, Ashok Nagar, Kharavela Nagar, Goutam Nagar, Budha Nagar, Madhusudan Nagar, Satya Nagar, Saheed Nagar etc. and different government residential colonies at unit-I, Unit-II, Unit-III, Unit-IV, Unit-V, Unit-VI, Unit-VII, Unit-VIII, and Unit-IX emerged with a high momentum that created favourable conditions for unswerving rise of floating population of rural poor who rushed into the city for wage-earning, rickshaw-pulling, etc. and also for doing some petty business. Subsequently, these people caused for the creation and growth of many slums in and around the city. When the Arise State Housing Board (OSHB) and Bhubaneswar Development Authority (BDA) were established and started promoting housing schemes for the people of various income groups and also started construction of a number of public and private sector commercial and official buildings, market complexes, parks etc., more and more rural wage-earning people of different parts of the state as well as of the neighbouring States immigrated into the city.

By the end of 1989, when a survey was made by Government of India for publishing a Town Directory for 1991 census, it is noticed that, there are 147 educational institutions including 75 primary schools, 25 junior secondary and middle schools, 26 matriculation/secondary schools/colleges, 5 higher secondary/Intermediate colleges, 2 engineering colleges, 1 polytechnic college, 2 medical colleges, and 11 degree level colleges excluding Utkal University (1943), Arise University of

Agriculture and Technology (1962), Regional College of Education, Regional Research laboratory, Institute of Physics, etc. The city has also 4 hospitals apart from a number of private sector hospitals and nursing homes and 22 dispensaries, 6 cinema halls, 6 auditoriums, 18 public libraries, 1 big stadium namely Kalinga Stadium, 41 banks and 29 agricultural and non-agricultural credit societies (cf. G.O.I, 1991: 3). In addition to the development of these infrastructures, Bhubaneswar city has also experienced growth of a number of hotels like Kalinga Ashok, Konark, Trident, Swosti, MayFair, Crown, Garden Inn, The Presidency and many others; State Museum, Planatorium, Kalinga Hospital, TV and Radio stations, New Bus Station, Railway Station, Airport etc. Recently, i.e. by the end of 2003, Bhubaneswar city has as many as 21 recognised privately managed Engineering colleges; some have their own buildings, and others are now constituting their buildings in and around the city.

All these urbanising features have originated during different periods of time, more particularly during the lapse of last three decades. Coinciding with development of the above urbanising features, growth of population in the city has also marched ahead abruptly.

Process of Urbanisation

As per the 1991 census, Bhubaneswar constitutes only 0.08 per cent of the total area (155707 kms) of Arise. But it comprises a total population of 411542 which account for 1.3 per cent of the total population of (31659736) of the state (Table—2.2).

There is a total number of 4 major class-I cities in the state namely, Berhampur, Bhubaneswar, Cuttack and Rourkela Steel Township which were provided with this status in 1971 or even before that depending upon their population size. But as per the data obtained through the last census work, Bhubaneswar is observed to be the most urbanising city in the state because of the reasons mentioned earlier. The growth of its population is much faster than the rest three cities. When one look at the figures presented in Table No. 2.1, it is revealed that in 1961, its population was only 38,211 but it increased to 1,05,491 in 1971,

2,19,211 in 1981 and 4,11,542 in 1991 census. Hence, the population of the city has crossed 4 lakh mark in the last census survey made in 1991. As a result of this, the growth rate during the decade of 1961-71, 1971-81 and 1981-91 come to be +176.07, +107.81 and +87.74 respectively. Thus, in each census year the growth rate of population in Bhubaneswar city is well high to the growth rate of other three cities. This is, of course, a phenomenal change because the city has special civic, religious, and administrative status.

When the growth rate of population in Bhubaneswar city is worked out for the last two decades as compared to the population of 1961 census, an amazing characteristic feature comes out into the fore. In 1961 the population of Bhubaneswar was very less as compared to the population of Berhampur, Cuttack and Rourkela, but interestingly during the decade of 1981-91, the city has experienced tremendous growth rate which is found to be 977.02 per cent. But in the rest three cities, during the lapse of last 30 years in between 1961-1991, the growth rate of population has been limited to below 200 per cent (Table—2.1).

Density of Population

Looking at the data available in Table No. 2.2, it can be said that during the last decade (1981-1991), the density of population per square kilometer in Bhubaneswar city has considerably increased. It was only 2359.39 in 1981 but it became 3299.21 in 1991 as against only 203 people per square kilometer of Arise. This means that during the lapse of 10 years in between 1981 to 1991, almost about an additional members of 940 have been accommodated in one sq. kilometer. This has undoubtedly given much pressure on the environment and on utilisation of the local resources. The density of population is much lower in the rest three cities.

Profile and Growth of Slums and Street Children in Bhubaneswar City

Housing and urban development documents show that during 1985, there were 69 slums in Bhubaneswar city (Mohanty and Acharya, 1990: 16-18). But as per the recent data (depending on the survey made in 1992) available in Bhubaneswar Municipality, this number has increased to as many as 101 slums. All these slums together constitute a total number of 18592 households and 73,930 population.

Of the total number of 101 slums, 37 (36.63%) are situated on *sthitiban** land. These slums have a total number of 2,766 (14.88%) households and 10,848 (14.67%) population. Apart from this, there are as many as 61 (60.34%) slums which are situated on encroached land and have a total number of 11598 (62.38%) households with a total number of 43,788 (59.23%) population. The rest 3 (3.97%) slums are resettlement colonies, namely sikharchandi, Dumuduma and Kokalandi which altogether constitute a total number of 4,242 (22.82%) households and 19,290 (26.09%) population (Table: 2.3). A detailed profile of each slums is presented in Appendix No. 2.

By now, we have concrete figures on the people living in different categories of slum in Bhubaneswar city but unfortunately, no effort has yet been made neither by any government nor by any NGO sector to find out the total households and population living on footpaths, railway platforms and bus terminals and also on the people who do not have any roof over their head. The condition of these people is quite appaling in the city.

However, if we break up the data presented in Appendix No. 2 into various smaller divisions of different dimensions, specific revelations come out into the picture.

Of the total 101 slums, maximum slums i.e., 41 or 40.59 per cent have 100 or less households followed by 36 or 35.64 per cent households that have 101-200 households. Nearly about 11 per cent slums have 201-300 households and the rest slums constitute less than 6 per cent of the total slums in each range of households. The average households per slum comes to be 184.22 (Table: 2.4).

---

* Status of a land held by a settled *raiyat* (resident) in a village (G.O.O., 1990: 526).

A further look at the same table also speaks that little more than 76 per cent slums constitute about 40 per cent of the total households and 39.46 per cent of the total population. But only 6 slums that fall in the last range, i.e. 501 and more households and 33.31 per cent of the total population. This is because of the fact that out of these 6 slums, 3 are rehabilitated colonies which altogether constitute a total number of 4,242 (22.80%) households of the total households of all the 101 slums.

When one looks into the Table No. 2.5, it is found that maximum number of slums, i.e. 53 (52.48%) have population of 500 or less followed by about 30 per cent slums having population in between 500-1000. But maximum households, i.e. 4,840 that constitute 26.03 per cent of the total 18,592 households of all the 101 slums are found in the population range of 501-1000. Still, more interestingly highest percentage (26.09%) of population of the total 73,930 come under the last population range i.e., 2001 and more who belong only to 3 or 2.97 per cent of the total number of slums. Irrespective of range of population size and number of slums, the average households size comes to be 4.

Status of Street Children in Bhubaneswar City

Conducting a scientific survey to estimate the exact number of street children in any city is a very difficult process because of a number of technical problems. So, no study has yet been undertaken by any government or Non-government organisations to find out the exact number of street children existing in Bhubaneswar city. However, out of a tentative estimation made after this study, it is expected that there would be nearly about 18,000 to 20,000 street children in the city who might be working in a wide range of activities.

Table—2.1: Growth of population in class-I cities in Orissa

Name of the city	*Population*				*Growth rate*		
	1961	*1971*	*1981*	*1991*	*1961-71*	*1971-81*	*1981-91*
Berhampur (Municipality)	76931	117662	162550	210418	+52.94	+38.15 (111.29)	+29.45 (173.51)
Bhubaneswar (Municipality)	38211	105491	219211	411542	+176.07	+107.81 (473.69)	+87.74 (977.02)
Cuttack (Municipality)	146308	205759	295268	397795	+32.64	+43.50 (101.81)	+34.72 (171.89)
Rourkela Steel Township (N.A.C.)	90287	125426	206821	215509	+38.92	64.49 (129.07)	4.20 (138.69)

Note: Figures in brackets indicate % age growth of population in different decades as compared to 1961.

Source: General Population Tables, Part-II-A, Series-19, Orissa, Census of India, 1991, pp. 549-591.

Table—2.2: Change of density of population in class I cities during 1981-1991

Name of the city	*Area (in Sq. Km.)*		*Population*		*Density*		
	1981	*1991*	*1981*	*1991*	*1981*	*1991*	*Difference*
Berhampur (Municipality)	76.15	79.80	162.550	210.418	2134.5	2636.82	502.32
Bhubaneswar (Municipality)	92.91	124.74	219221	411542	2359.39	3299.21	939.82
Cuttack (Municipality)	59.57	91.36	269950	397795	4531.65	4354.15	-177.49
Rourkela Steel Township (NAC)	121.73	121.73	206821	215509	1699.01	1770.39	71.38

Source: General Population Tables, Part-II-A, Series-19, Orissa, Census of India, 1991, pp. 549-591.

Table—2.3: Category of slums in Bhubaneswar city

Category	*Total slums*	*Total households*	*% age*	*Total population*	*% age*
Slums in *sthitiban* land	37 (36.63)	2760	14.85	10,848	14.67
Slum in encroached land	61 (60.4)	11590	62.34	43792	59.23
Rehabilitated colonies	3 (2.97)	4242	22.82	19290	26.09
Total	**101**	**18592**	**100.0**	**73930**	**100.0**

Note: Figures in brackets represent % age.

Source: Calculated from the data available in BMC, 1997.

Table—2.4: Socio-economic profile of slums in Bhubaneswar municipality corporation

Range of households	*Total No. of slums*	*% age to total slums*	*Total households*	*% age to total households*	*AV. households per slums*	*Total population*	*% age to total population*
<100	41	40.59	2339	12.57	57.05	9649	13.05
101-200	36	35.64	5075	27.28	140.97	19527	26.41
201-300	11	10.89	2796	15.03	254.18	10980	14.85
301-400	6	5.94	2054	11.11	344.67	7549	10.21
401-500	1	0.99	459	2.47	459	1597	2.16
501 and more	6	5.94	5868	31.54	978.17	24628	33.31
Total	**101**	**100.0**	**18592**	**100.0**	**184.22**	**73930**	**100.0**

Source: Calculated from the data available in BMC, 1997.

Table—2.5: Population range and household size in slums

Range of population	*Total slums*	*Total households*	*Total population*	*Household size*
<500	53 (52.48)	3875 (20.84)	14735 (19.93)	3.80
501-1000	30 (29.70)	4840 (26.03)	19662 (26.60)	4.06
1001-1500	9 (8.91)	2700 (14.52)	10134 (3.71)	3.75
1501-2000	6 (5.94)	2835 (15.25)	10109 (13.67)	3.57
2001 and more	3 (2.97)	4242 (22.82)	19290 (26.09)	4.55
Total	**101** **(100.00)**	**18592** **(100.00)**	**73930** **(100.00)**	**4.0**

Note: Figures in brackets represent % age.

Source: Calculated from the data available in BMC, 1997.

3

Family Milieu

Family is a small and primary social unit where the children take birth and are nourished and socialised. Beginning from their childhood, they are trained on what to do, how to do and what not to do. Instructions are regularly given to them about earning of their livelihood in future. Thus, development of personality and their future career absolutely depends on their family background; more specifically on the extent of education, level of awareness and working conditions of their parents. When their parents are poor, illiterate and earn their livelihood out of unskilled and unspecified wage-earning sources or even out of unsalaried jobs, normally their children also remain illiterate and subsequently become unskilled wage-earners. Owing to this, there is hardly any person in any society having good personality and a high rank who has come up into the mainstream out of confuting and disharmonious family situations.

When the rural people migrate to accessible urban areas in order to gain regular income, their familial set-up is severely disturbed because of an improper and irregular or mal adaptation in the new socio-economic, ecological and cultural niche. Their first and foremost aim concentrates on 'how to sustain life'. In such a demanding situation, they forget to give much importance on the education of their children rather they like to engage them in any work from which they can earn their own daily bread and butter and contribute something to improve the economy of their family. At an age, when a child should attend school for building up his/her career, but fails to do so and takes to some painstaking task of earning daily against his/her will and psycho-physical maturity, his/her life turns up into a different world of uncertain plight.

With this backdrop image, the family background of the street children is being discussed below. Their specific socio-economic, educational, and other situational characteristics shall be discussed in a greater detail in the next chapter.

Immigration

Table No. 3.1 illustrates the data relating to immigration of the parents of the street children into Bhubaneswar city. It is observed that the parents of all the 120 sample street children have come into the city from three neighbouring states excluding Orissa. Since Bhubaneswar city is situated within the state of Orissa as its capital, it has pulled thousands of rural poor from different parts of the state. As per the present findings, as many as in 79 or 65.83 per cent of cases, the parents of the street children have come from different districts of Orissa, namely Balasore, Bhadrak, Cuttack, Gajapati, Ganjam, Jagatsingpur, Kendrapada, Khurdha, Nayagarh, Nawapara, and Sambalpur. But surprisingly maximum number (37) of parents accounting for 30.83 per cent of the total cases have come from the district of Ganjam alone followed by Nayagarh, Balasore and Cuttack with 5.83 per cent each and Bhadrak with 5 per cent. Less than 3.5 per cent of cases have immigrated from the other districts. There is only one case which is found to be a permanent resident of the Bhubaneswar city itself.

So far as immigration from the neighbouring states is concerned, maximum parents (26 or 21.67%) have come from West Bengal (Medinapur-16.67%, Kharagpur-33% and Calcutta city 1.67%) followed by Andhra Pradesh that has pushed a total number of 10 cases into the above city. These 10 case account for 8.33 per cent of the total sample. Further fragmentation of these cases, show that while 4.17 and 2.5 per cent of cases have come from Srikakulum and Ichhapur respectively, the rest 1.67 per cent have come from Vijayawada district. There is only one child in which case its, parents are found to have come from the state of Bihar.

Duration of Staying in Bhubaneswar City

When one looks at the Table No. 3.2, it is revealed that in case of a high percentage (24.17%) of the parents of the street children, the length of saying in Bhubaneswar city is 21 years or even more followed by 17.5 per cent of cases who have come into the city in between 6-10 years ago, 15.83 per cent of cases just before 5 years or less, 13.33 per cent of cases before 16-20 years and 11.67 per cent before 11-15 years. The rest 17.5 per cent of street children do not know about the length of their staying in the city.

Family Size

Most often quality of life (QOL) depends on the family size and income level of the family. If the family size is large but the income is low, the family members are supposed to face a number of hazards, like lack of required nutritional input; it causes improper physical and mental growth of children, lack of clothing; the child is more frequently exposed to sun, rain, and cold etc. His/her personality is truncated due to lack of education and thereby the foundation of the future of the child is weakened and so on so fourth. As a result, one must taken much precaution to limit its family size only to 3 or 4. But the present study speaks that only in 18.33 per cent of cases, the family size is limited to this ideal number. On the contrary a total number of 49 households, accounting for about 41 per cent, have 5.6 per cent, have 5.6 members followed by 25 per cent of households having 7-8 members. The rest 15 per cent of households have very large family size that is 9 or more per household. Thus, about 66 per cent of households are found to have 5-8 members per household, and if 5 is considered as a cut off point, little more than 80 per cent of households are found to have 5 or more members per family. Still then it is not a surprising social characteristics feature of the slum dwellers. Because these people like to relax themselves more through sexual amusement with their partners and consider the children born to them as the gift of the God. These children are also considered as economic assets for the family and the family feels proud to have more children.

The total family members of all the 120 sample street children come to 761 with an average family size of 6.34 per household (Table: 3.3).

Education of the Parents

The extent of educational achievement of the parents of the street children is very poor. There are only about 13 per cent of fathers who are found to the literate (primary-7.5%, middle-1.67%, upto high school or under matric-1.67% and matriculation or above-0.8%) as against only merely 3 per cent of the mothers (primary-1.67%, upto high school but under matric-0.83% and matriculation or more-0.83%). This otherwise means that as many as about 97 per cent of mothers of the street children are illiterate as against 87 per cent of fathers (Table: 3.4).

Total Literate Households and Population

There is a universally accepted usage that reads as 'if you educate a woman, you educate a family but if you educate a man you educate a person'. Hence as in this case the education level of the parents of the street children in general and their mothers in particular is very poor, it has created an insignificant impact on the educational development of their children. In this respect Table No. 3.5 depicts that of the total number of 761 population of the total 120 households only 94 persons or 12.35 per cent are found to be literate.

When one further looks into the same table it is observed that there are a total number of only 41 (31.17%) literate households*. In case of the rest 79 (65.83%) households, there is not a single person who is literate. The above table also indicates that the literate households constitute only 94 (12.35%) population and the rest population i.e., 667 (84.65%) belong to the illiterate households of which not a single person is able to read, write and to work out simple arithmetic calculations with understanding.

If we further break up the literate households according to the number of literate persons available, it can be observed from the Table No. 3.6 that in case of 29 or 70.73 per cent of households, there are 1-2 literate persons, followed by 7 (17.67%)

---

* A household that constitutes atleast one literate person is considered as a literate household. Conversely a household that does not consist any literate person, it is considered as an illiterate household.

households having 3-4 such persons. The rest 5 (12.20%) households have 5-6 literate persons. Further the Table No. 3.7 speaks that even though there are 41 literate households, in case of only 2 households (4.88%), the highest educational qualification achieved by some members of the family is found to be only matriculation.

Interestingly merely class IV is found to be the highest educational qualification achieved by some members of highest number of households, i.e., 8 or 19.51 per cent of the total literate households.

Occupation of Family Members

Occupation of the family members of the street children are discussed below separately for parents and children and the street children who are interviewed as subjects are included in the children category.

Occupation of Fathers

A perusal of the Table No. 3.8 makes it visible that the parents of the street children mostly earn their livelihood out of various unlucrative occupations. Majority of them (29.36%) work as wage-earner or coolie followed by 23.85 per cent who earn their livelihood out of rickshaw and trolley pulling. There are 15.60 per cent of them who concentrate on purchase of rags from different colonies, and sell those with profit. Some also collect rags from street or garbage heaps and sell those at the local rag godowns. Some well-to-do slum residents purchase rags from rag-pickers at their house-sites and dispose off their collection at the end of every weak or when they want to do so, to the total rag dealers at a profitable rate (Appendix: 3).

As a number of buildings are being constructed day by day in Bhubaneswar city and there is a great demand for construction labourers, many of them have felt its importance and have taken to this occupation. It is found that a total number of 9 (8.26%) household heads (fathers) of the street children have developed specialised skills on this sector and have taken to masonry.

A significant part (5.5%) of the total sample resort to extract profit out of vending of various edible items, like milk or milk products (1 or 0.92%), fruits, like banana, orange, apple, pears etc. (3 or 2.75%), drinks, like green coconut (1 or 0.92%) and various ornaments and cosmetics like ear-ring, hair-pins, necklaces toe-rings etc. (1 or 0.92%) at various business centres like railway stations, bus stations, market complexes, parking areas etc. An equal percentage of them earn their livelihood out of shoe-shining, shoe repairing and also from shoe manufacturing followed by 2.75 per cent with shop keeping and 1.83 per cent with beggary. Surprisingly, out of the total sample there is only one household head (0.92%) who is found to serve in an organised sector but his service is temporary in tenure. One household head (0.92%) performs monkey-show followed by another household head who has taken to the occupation of coconut plucking in the city. The rest one household head is a skilled painter and he has acquired the skill in Bhubaneswar city.

Occupation of Mothers

The occupations of working mothers have been categorised into seven groups. These are: wage-earnings, rag-picking, domestic service (maid servant) vending, service in organised sector, beggary and house management (housewife). But of the total 107 cases, as many as 46 mothers constituting 42.99 per cent are engaged in wage-earning apart from domestic routine, followed by 20 or 18.69 per cent, in rag-picking, 17 or 15.89 per cent in domestic service (maid servant), 2 or 1.87 per cent in vending of steel utensils and fruits, and 1 or 0.93 per cent in an organised sector. A large number of mothers, i.e. 20 who account for 18.69 per cent of the total sample do not go out of their home to work as wage-earners or to earn from any other sources rather they manage their home as house-wives. This section mainly belongs to Mochi, a Scheduled Caste community. Comparatively their economic condition is little better than other slum dwellers as their male family members earn out of their own informal household industry, i.e. shoe-repairing which also includes other related activities, like shoe-shining at road sides, market complexes, railway platforms, but stations and also at some other important localities.

Occupation of Brothers

Occupation of one brother has a great impact on another. Particularly elder brothers are more influential for the younger brothers as younger ones always try to imitate their elder brothers. Hence, when the elder brother plays, the younger brother cannot keep quiet and confine himself to study. Likewise, when the elder brother wakes up early in the morning, picks up his sack and goes out of home to collect rags from the streets, his younger brother runs after him and extends his hand to collect the same with his brother even if he does not know its meaning, importance or significance. After he becomes aware of the situation, he raises his own money out of it. However, parents also regularly instruct him to keep up the habit and they keep their eyes on his daily earning, a major part of which is spend towards the management of the whole family. In this context when we compare the occupations of the street children with the occupation of their brothers, almost a common feature come into the fore.

Table No. 3.10 reflects that of the total 292 brothers, as many as 128 comprising 43.84 per cent of the total sample collect rags followed by 22 or 7.53 per cent who are engaged in collection of potato from different potato godown compounds located at Ainginia. A total number of 16 of them accounting for more than 5 per cent (5.48%) work in different motor cycle garages and cycle repairing shops followed by 15 or 5.14 per cent who earn their livelihood out of shoe shining and shoe-repairing business. Further, 13 or 4.45 per cent earn from rickshaw and trolley pulling. They are followed by 12 or 4.11 per cent who work in the sector of wage earning. Little less than 3 per cent (2.74%) or a total number of 8 of them vend various edible items, like sweets, fruits, groundnut, cold drinks, mineral water, betel and smokes, etc. at various places, the main being the railway platform. About 2 per cent constituting a total number of 6 of them work as hotel boys and 1.36 per cent or 4 of them practise domestic service. An equal percentage of them concentrate on cleaning of railway platforms, train compartments etc. and collect some tips and alms from the passengers. Slightly more than 1 per cent (1.03) or 3 of them are engaged in potato sorting at different potato shops in daily and weekly markets. An equal per cent work as sales boys at different grocery shops. A group of 2 of them have gained the skill of construction works and have become masons. Another group consisting of same number of them practice a specialised business, i.e., sharpening of cutting tools, like scissors, knives, bill-looks etc., through mechanical devices.

About 5 per cent of brothers of the street children are either unemployed or because of some other reasons, remain at home and look after younger siblings as baby-sitters.

Amongst the rest, there are 18 brothers who are under the age of 5 years and 4 brothers accounting for 1.37 per cent of the total sample are disabled or diseased who are unable to do any work. The remaining 12 or 4.11 per cent of brothers are students who are now continuing education in different formal or non-formal educational institutions.

Occupation of Sisters

There are 205 sisters of all the street children studied. Most of them, i.e., 85 accounting for more than 40 per cent (41.46%) are engaged in the business of rag-picking. They are followed by 38 or 18.54 per cent of maid servants and 15 or 7.32 per cent of wage-earners. Amongst the rest, 12 or 5.85 per cent sort out potato at different shops, 7 or 3.41 per cent collect potato from the sites of potato godowns, 4 or 1.95 per cent collect semi-burnt coal and green coconut fibres for fuel and selling purpose, 2 or 0.98 per cent work as hotel assistants and only 1 of them consisting of 0.49 per cent cleans the railway platforms and the train compartments.

A total number of 12 or 5.85 per cent of them look after their younger brothers and sisters at home when their parents are away.

There are 9 (4.39%) sisters who are found under the age of 5 years and the remaining 15 (7.32%) are now continuing education as regular students in formal and non-formal educational institutions.

Table—3.1: Migration status of street children in Bhubaneswar city

Sl. No.	State/district	Total migrants	Percentage	Remarks
(1)	(2)	(3)	(4)	(5)
1.	**Andhra Pradesh**	10	8.33	–
	(i) Ichhapur	5	4.17	–
	(ii) Srikakulum	3	2.5	–
	(iii) Vijayawada	2	1.67	–
2.	**Bihar**	1	0.83	Silcher village-1
3.	**Orissa**	79	65.83	–
	(i) Balasore	7	5.83	Soro-7
	(ii) Bhadrak	2	1.67	Bhadrak-1 Akhandalamani-1
	(iii) Bhubaneswar	1	0.83	Samantarapur village-1
	(iv) Cuttack	7	5.83	Choudwar-1, Narasinghpur-1, Cuttack town-2 Salepur-2
	(v) Gajapati	3	2.5	Gajapati-1 Paralakhemundi-2
	(vi) Ganjam	37	30.83	Chikiti-2, Aska-16 Ganjam-110, Berhampur-18 Bhanjanager-2, Chhatrapur-3

(Contd...)

(1)	(2)	(3)	(4)	(5)
	(vii) Jagatsingpur	1	0.83	Jagatsigpur-1
	(viii) Kendrapada	2	1.67	Salepur-2
	(ix) Khurdha	6	5.0	Khurdha-4, Taraboi-2
	(x) Nayagarh	7	5.83	–
	(xi) Nayapara	4	3.33	Nayapara-4
	(xii) Sambalpur	1	0.83	Ichhapali-1
4.	**West-Bengal**	26	21.67	–
	(i) Calcutta city	2	1.67	–
	(ii) Khadagpur	4	3.33	–
	(iii) Medinapur	20	16.67	–
	Do not know/No answer	4	3.33	–
	Total	**120**	**100.0**	–

Table—3.2: Duration of staying in Bhubaneswar city

Range of year (1)	*Total cases* (2)	*Percentage* (3)
<5	19	15.83
6-10	21	17.5
11-15	14	11.67
16-20	16	13.33
21+	29	24.17
Do not know/No answer	21	17.5
Total	**120**	**100.0**

Table—3.3: Family size and population

Family size	*Total household*	*% age*	*Total population*	*% age*	*Average family size*
1-2	1	0.83	2	0.26	2.0
3-4	22	18.33	87	11.43	3.95
5-6	49	40.83	273	35.87	5.57
7-8	30	25.00	223	29.30	7.43
9 and more	18	15.00	176	23.13	9.77
Total	**120**	**100.00**	**761**	**100.00**	**6.34**

Table—3.4: Educational status of parents

Level of education	*Fathers*	*% age*	*Mothers*	*% age*
Illiterate	104	86.67	116	96.67
Primary (I-IV)	9	7.5	2	1.67
Middle (VI-VII)	2	1.67	–	–
High school but below matriculation (VIII-X)	2	1.67	1	0.83
Matriculation	1	0.83	1	0.83
Total	**120**	**100.00**	**120**	**100.00**

Note: *(i)* Those who have passed H.S.C. Exam are included in Matriculation.

(ii) Absolute figures also include those fathers and mothers who are not alive.

Table—3.5: Total literature households according to population

Category of population according to level of education	*Total*	*% age*	*Total persons*	*% age*
Households having atleast one literate person	41	34.17	94	12.35
Households having no literate person	79	65.83	667	87.65
Total	**120**	**100.00**	**761**	**100.0**

Table—3.6: Range of total literature persons according to number of households

Range of literates (in no. of persons)	*Total households*	*% age to total*	*Total population*	*% age to total literate population*
1-2	29	70.73	46	48.94
3-4	7	17.07	22	23.40
5-6	5	12.20	26	27.66
Total	**41**	**100.00**	**94**	**100.00**

Table—3.7: Highest educational qualification achieved among persons in literature households

Class	*Total households*	*% age*
1st	4	9.76
2nd	4	9.76
3rd	6	14.63
4th	8	19.51
5th	4	9.76
6th	6	14.67
7th	3	7.31
8th	2	4.88
9th	2	4.88
10th	2	4.88
Total	**41**	**100.00**

Table—3.8: Occupation of households heads (Fathers)

Sl. No.	*Occupation*	*Total cases*	*% age*	*Remarks*
1.	Beggary	2	1.83	–
2.	Coconut plucking	1	0.92	–
3.	Masonry	9	8.26	–
4.	Mechanic/helper at garages	4	3.67	–
5.	Monkey-show	1	0.92	–
6.	Painter	1	0.92	House colour mistry-1
7.	Rag-picking/purchasing/godown keeping	17	15.60	Rag-picking-3 (2.75%) Rag purchasing-11 (10.09%) Rag godown keeping-3 (2.75%)
8.	Rickshaw/trolley pulling	26	23.85	–
9.	Service in organised sector	1	0.92	NMR Peon-1
10.	Shoe-shining	6	5.50	–
11.	Shop-keeping	3	2.75	Tea shop-3
12.	Vending	6	5.50	Selling of green coconut-1, Banana and fruits-3, ornaments-1 milk and milk product-1
13.	Wage-earning/coolie	32	29.36	–
	Total	**109**	**100.00**	–

Note: Total figure does not include those fathers who are not alive.

Table—3.9: Occupation of mothers

Sl. No.	Occupation	Total cases	% age	Remarks
1.	Beggary	1	0.93	
2.	House wife	20	18.69	
3.	Maid servant	17	15.89	
4.	Rag-picking	20	18.69	
5.	Service in organised sector	1	0.93	NMR peon-1
6.	Vending	2	1.87	Steel utensils-1 banana and other fruits-1
7.	Wage-earning/coolie	46	42.99	
	Total	**107**	**100.00**	

Table—3.10: Occupation of brothers

Sl. No.	Occupation	Total cases	% age
1.	Domestic servant	34	1.36
2.	Garage boy/asst. at cycle repairing shop	16	5.48
3.	Hotel boy	6	2.05
4.	Masonry	2	0.68
5.	Potato collection	22	7.53
6.	Potato sorting	3	1.03
7.	Radio mechanic	1	0.34
8.	Rag-picking		
9.	Railway platform and train compartment cleaning	4	1.36
10.	Rickshaw/trolley pulling	13	4.45
11.	Sales boy at grocery shop	3	1.03
12.	Sharpening of cutting instruments	2	0.68
13.	Shoe-shining	15	5.14
14.	Tailoring	5	1.71
15.	Vending	8	2.74
16.	Wage-earning	12	4.11
17.	Watching younger siblings at home	14	4.79
A	Brothers below the age of 5 years old	18	6.16
B	Disabled/patient/diseased	4	1.37
C	Student	12	4.11
	Total	**292**	**100.00**

Note: Total figure includes the subjects (street children).

Table—3.11: Occupation of sisters

Sl. No.	*Occupation*	*Total cases*	*% age*
1.	Beggary	7	3.411
2.	Collection of semi-burnt coal and greet coconut fibres	4	1.95
3.	Hotel Asst.	2	0.98
4.	Maid servant	38	18.54
5.	Potato collection	5	2.44
6.	Potato sorting	12	5.85
7.	Rag-picking	85	41.46
8.	Railway platform and train compartment cleaning	1	0.49
9.	Wage-earning	15	7.32
10.	Watching of younger sibling at home	12	5.85
A	Sisters below the age of 5 years old	9	4.39
B	Student	15	7.32
	Total	**205**	**100.00**

Note: Total figure includes the subjects (street children).

4

Socio-Economic Profile of the Street Children

Poor and disharmonious family conditions and unconductive socio-economic factors that have been responsible to push a number of children into the streets of Bhubaneswar city, are discussed in the preceding chapter as the backdrop information of the sample street children. In the present chapter, a vivid picture of these children is analysed below taking the following broad variables into consideration.

Category of Street Children

The sample street children can broadly be divided into 4 categories depending upon the place of residence of their parents or guardians. They are those, whose parents are staying (i) under abandoned or incomplete constructions, (ii) in basti/slums or villages, (iii) at railway platforms/bus stations etc., and (iv) on pavements. But the children whose parents or guardians live in different bastis/slums or villages (Appendix: 4) are found to be maximum, i.e. 106 or 88.33 per cent, followed by 12 or 10 per cent of children whose parents stay under various abandoned or semi-constructed building. There is only one street child whose parents have constructed their house on pavement. The parents of the rest one child have not constructed any house at any place in the city rather spend their nights at local railway platforms and bus stations depending upon their choice and interest (Table: 4.1).

The street children belonging to these four categories may or may not be staying with their parents. So, if the basis of availability of suitable shelter to them and their contact with their parents are considered, these children can be put into 3 limited categories, viz. (i) *children on the street*, (ii) *children of the street* and (iii) *abandoned/orphan or neglected children*.

A detailed picture on these 3 categories of children is presented in Table No. 4.2 which reflects that maximum street children fall in the first category, i.e. *'children on the street'* who constitute as many as 106 children accounting for little less than 90 per cent (89.17%) of the total sample of 120.

This category of children more or less keep regular contact with their parents and come back to their respective homes or parents at the end of each working day. Very few of them attend formal or non-formal educational institutions. They consider their parents as guardians and also obey them. They have a sense of belongingness to their own natal family, community and basti or village. These children are to give a major portion of their daily income to their parents either voluntarily or by force applied by their parents or guardians towards the management of kitchen of their families. If they do not contribute the same, they are often scolded, beaten up, given less or no food and at times they are also not allowed to enter into the house. These torturing and depressing situations put them in desperate situations and in that situation they come out of their homes to lead their life independent. In the long run, repetition of this situation gives birth to the second category of street children, i.e. 'children of the street'.

The second category of street children constitute 10 per cent or a total number of 12 street children. These children consider the street, that may be a railway platform, abandoned house, incomplete building, garage, hotel, market complex premise, pavement or any other such place as their home. They keep very less contact with their respective homes or family members. They earn for themselves but occasionally give some part of their income to their parents or to the family members if they like to do so. If they are again ill-treated by their family members during their 'infrequent' visits, they feel more frustrated and disgusted than before and linger the gap of time for their next visit. They have very slight sense of belongingness to their own natal family, community, basti/slum or village.

The last category of children are found in a very small proportion i.e. only with 2 cases (1.67%). These children in some way are an extension of the second category. But the situation of these children is more serious than those of the second category. Because they are either abandoned by their parents or are orphans or are neglected by their guardians (in case of orphans), like the above category, they also lead independent life and stay alone at railway platforms, market complex premises, pavements or any other such places depending on the availability of space and their choice. They are in one sense considered as 'thrown out children', and hence they lack any sense of belongingness to their natal family, community, basti/ slum or village. They earn for themselves, and share the essence of family with their peers or with the family members of their peers who act as their partners, supporters, instructors etc. during hazardous situations.

Demographic Structure

Table No. 4.3 describes age structure of these children according to different age groups. As mentioned earlier in the last chapter the sample of street children has been selected keeping in view that they are below the age of 14 years in case of either sexes. The whole sample has been classified into 4 age groups, viz, 7-8, 9-10, 11-12 and 13-14.

It is observed that most of the street children (35%) irrespective of sex fall in the age group of 13-14 but interestingly when majority (36.67%) of the girl street children are found in the age group of 9-10, maximum percentage of boy street children come in the age group of 13-14. This apparently indicates that in lower age groups, the work participation of the girl street children is higher than those of the boy street children. This is because of the fact that when girls attain adolescence or puberty they feel unsafe to work on streets. As a result the parents of the grown up girls try to engage them in some other works where they are safe and are secured.

Place of Birth

Place of birth of the street children is considered important to know about the spatial mobility of their parents and approximate duration of staying in a particular place of work. In this respect, it may be noticed from Table No. 4.4 that of the total sample, exactly 35 per cent or 42 street children have taken their birth in Bhubaneswar city itself and have been brought up in the city. But as many as 74 (61.67%) of them are born outside the city and then their parents have come over to Bhubaneswar city. The rest 3.33 per cent of children do not know about the place of their birth.

Religion, Community and Caste

The religious background of the street children is reflected in Table No. 4.5 which indicates that most of these children (70.83%) belong to Hindu religion followed by 22.5 per cent of Muslims and the rest 6.67 per cent do not belong to any philosophical religion. They are tribal and as much they are animists.

In furtherance to this, the next table shows information about the linguistic communal affiliation of the street children. If the Urdus (Muslims) and the Tribals are excluded, it is found that a total number 38 or 31.67 per cent of children are Oriya backward caste Hindus followed by 30 or 25 per cent Telugu, 13 or 10.83 per cent Scheduled Castes and 3 or 2.5 per cent Tamils. The rest 1 (0.83%) child belongs to the Bengali linguistic family (Table 4.6).

When the community-wise street children are further broken up by castes, it is observed that most of the street children (79 or 65.83%) are not able to speak about their caste affiliation as it is beyond their knowledge. However, the rest who could tell about their castes, comprise 9.17 per cent of *Matia* whose traditional caste based occupation in earth cutting. Next to them are the *Mochi* (cobbler) who are represented by 8.33 per cent of the total sample. They are followed by 6.67 per cent of *Sabara*, a tribal community who traditionally earn their livelihood out of agriculture, hunting and gathering. Following the *Sabara*, the

Gauda (cattle herder) people comprise 5 per cent of the total sample. The rest castes are *Barika* (Barbar) and *Chasa/Khandayat*, each of them constitutes less than 2 per cent followed by *Kumbhara* (potter) and *Tanti* (Weaver) each constituting 0.83 per cent of the total sample (Table 4.7).

Living Parents and Shelter of Street Children

Economic pressure on the street children is reasonably much high compared to any other children. But when the parents, particularly fathers of these children are died, economic pressure is mounted on them unexpectedly and in that case they are to spend more time on the streets to earn more as a responsible earner of the family. The given data in Table No. 4.8, show that in case of 8.33 per cent of street children, their fathers are not alive followed by 5.83 per cent who have lost their mothers. One child (0.83%) is found to be an orphan. The rest 85 per cent of street children fortunately have both the parents.

Shelter

The street children who belong to the first category, i.e. "children on the street" are living with their parents but in some cases when space at home is not sufficient, they may, at times spend their night at the community hall. They are not allowed to spend their nights at railway platforms, bus stations or at any other such places. But the children of the second and third categories are found to spend nights mostly at railway platforms, market complex premises, bus stations. As given in Table No. 9, the data show that a total number of 7 street children accounting for 5.83 per cent, regularly stay in railway platforms, followed by 1.67 per cent who stay at different market complex premises. Another group of street children accounting for 1.67 per cent are living in abandoned or dilapidated houses. An equal percentage of children are there who have taken different garages or hotel premises as their regular shelter. The rest one child has been able to manage itself to stay with its relatives' house.

Duration of Staying on Street/outside Home

So far as the duration of living outside the home is concerned, among the total cases of 14 street children who have left their home and are staying at various insecured places, a total number of 6 (43%) children have been staying outside their home for 3 or more years followed by 35.71 per cent who have left their respective homes in between 1-2 years and are staying at some places of their own choices. There are 3 or 21.43 per cent of street children who have very recently left their homes and have been staying on streets from the last year (Table 4.10).

Causes for Staying on Street/outside Home

The factors responsible for staying outside home among the 'children of the street' and 'abandoned or orphan or neglected' are attributed to a total number of 6 reasons. The reason of staying outside home among each of the children of these two categories is not merely confined to only one factor rather in some cases it is more than that. As a result multiple reasons are found responsible for this.

Looking at the Table No. 4.11, one can observe that maximum children (64.29%) have left home and are staying on streets because of their anguish, suffering, torture and regular conflict with their parents. This happens when they fail to work as per the instructions of their parents and requirement of home. More particularly, conflicting situations arise when the child does not give a major part of its daily income to its parents. Another reason which is attributed in 28.57 per cent of cases is 'broken family'. Next to this reason, availability of easy income opportunities at railway platforms seems to be an important factor for attracting children to stay over there or in other words outside their homes. Little more than 21 per cent (21.43%) of children opine that they have left their homes and are permanently staying at railway platforms as the place is very resourceful and is more yielding than staying at home and doing jobs, like picking of scraps or doing any other similar activity. About 14 per cent of children explain that they have come out of their homes because of death of their parents (father or mother or both). An equal number of them justify that the space available at their home is not sufficient for all the family members to be accommodated. This has resulted them to come out of their homes and to lead independent life at some places on streets. These children earn for themselves and since they keep very less contact with their parents, they spend their income independently. Further an equal percentage of these children opine that they are to stay outside of their homes because of their late night working pattern, i.e. working in hotels and garages (Table: 4.9) which require their attendance from early morning to late night.

Educational Status of Street Children

Street children are deprived of their right to education. As a result, educationally they remain very backward. Still then the rate of their literacy (Table: 4.12) is found to be little higher than their parents (Table: 3.4) because of generational advantage. However, the former table describes that about 78 per cent of street children are found to be illiterate as against the rest 22 per cent being literates. But the highest educational level achieved by most of the literate street children is observed to be only primary standard, i.e. from class I to class V. Merely 2 of them have passed middle school education that covers from class VI to class VII. However, fortunately only one street child has been able to reach high school education, i.e., from class VII to class X but unluckily has failed to complete High School Certificate (HSC) examination.

Continuing Education Among the Street Children

It is surprising to note that even though the street children are to spend most of their time on streets, a total number of 5 (4.17%) of them are still continuing formal education apart from working regularly on streets. More interestingly there are 26 children (21.67%) who are enrolled in different Non-Formal-Education (NFE) centres run by some nodal state level Non-Government-Organisation (NGOs) in the city. But they do not attend these institutions with the actual purpose of being educated and get employed in future rather they attend these institutions to get some nutritional incentives that are provided to them at the end of all classes everyday. On personal observation and on discussion with the street children and also with the project administrators, street educators etc. it comes to the notice that they are very irregular in attending such institutions because of a wide range of interrelated reasons. Most of them work on streets and reach at their respective NFE centres at the time of distribution of nutritional stuffs that include banana, bread etc. If the educators deny them their share, they become mischievous and create problems. It is quite natural for them to react in such a way as the need of education is secondary for them.

Occupation of Street Children

Generally, the street children take to such occupations that do not require any formal education and hence are easily approachable by them. They do not bother about the social and religious sanctity of the job they adopt and mind less for their social prestige in the public. Hunger, the most serious propelling instinct that may compel a child to beg alms or even to snatch food from the mouth of an animal but he/she does not generally adopt such occupations that are not approved by his/her parents or guardians. Still then a Muslim rag-picker (boy) whose situation become crucial when he fails to earn his livelihood out of this, may extend his unskilled hand for polishing shoes at the shop of his Mochi (cobbler) friend. But he never reveals this fact to his parents. On the other hand a Mochi shoe-shiner can never go for picking rags willingly even if his stomach is empty. He feels it derogatory as a result he may like to adopt some other occupations according to his own choice. Likewise, a barber-vendor at the railway platform hesitates to hold a whisk to clean the platform or train compartments. But he can jump over to any world depending upon his personal choice and interest with the permission of their parents. But if he is independent and has less or no contact with his parents, he enjoys absolute freedom to earn out of any type of work of his own interest and choice which may be rag-picking, shoe-shining, collection of rotten fruits, sorting of vegetables, cleaning of utensils at hotels or washing of clothes as a domestic servant etc. Thus, a child of the street can take to any kind of sundry job depending on his personal situation and interest.

The present study reveals that the street children of Bhubaneswar city are engaged in as many as 10 different occupations. These are (1) collection of semi-burnt coal and green coconut fibres, (2) domestic service (3) garage work and working in cycle-repairing shops, (4) menial work in hotels (5) potato collection (6) potato sorting (7) rag-picking (8) cleaning of railway platforms and train compartments and collection of tips, alms etc., (9) shoe-shining and (10) vending of edible items at various market complexes, railway stations and public places. But surprisingly most of the street children (55.83%) are engaged in rag-picking followed by about 12 per cent of them engaged in collection of potato from different potato godown sites at Ainginia area. Next to them, 8.33 per cent are found to work as domestic servants. An equal percentage of these children are observed to be self-employed with the business of shoe-shining at railway platforms, bus stations, footpaths etc. A total number of 7 of them accounting for 5.83 per cent work in different automobile garages, work-shops and cycle-repairing shops followed by 3.33 per cent engaged in vending of various edible items, like egg, ground-nut, betel and cigarette, tea etc. at railway platforms and in train compartments. Only 2 of them (1.67%) collect thrown out semi-burnt coal from tea shops and hotel sites and green coconut fibres from road sides for selling or for personal use as fuel. Another group consisting of an equal number of street children work as hotel assistants. Further same number of these children to sort out potatoes of different grades and rotten potatoes and potato godowns and potato shops. The rest 2 street children are found to clean railway platforms and train compartments and beg for tips, alms etc. (Table: 4.14).

A cursory look at the same table also reveals sex-wise distribution of occupation of these children. It is observed that in case of either sexes, adoption of rag-picking is found to be highest that comes to 57.58 per cent for the boys as against 50 per cent girls. But so far as the next important occupation is concerned, when it is, potato collection (13.33%) for boys, it is domestic service (30.00%) for the girls.

Linguistic Community and Occupation

Community and caste play important roles in defining one's occupation both in rural Indian society as well as in urban centres. The system is more rigid in rural societies. Change of traditional caste based occupations is difficult, expecting the ritually pure and neutral ones, but it is not so in urban areas. Here, the people conceal their caste identity and exercise greater flexibility to adopt and specialise in various jobs according to their own choice and profitability. In this context the data presented in Table No. 4.15 illustrate some existing features. Interestingly the Scheduled Tribe (ST) street children work only in 2 sectors, viz domestic service (62.5%) and rag-picking (37.5%), the Scheduled Castes (SC) also in 2 sectors, viz shoe-shining (76.92%) and rag-picking (23.08%), Oriya backward caste Hindu as many as in 6 sectors, viz collection of potato from godown sites (36.84%), rag-picking (36.84%), vending of edible items (10.53%), domestic service (5.26%), working in automobile garages, workshop and cycle repairing shops (5.26%) and hotels (5.26%), Urdu speaking children or Muslims in 4 sectors, viz rag-picking (88.89%) working in automobile garages, work-shops and cycle repairing shops (3.7%), cleaning of railway platforms and train compartments (3.7%), and potato sorting and grading (3.7%), Telugu children in 6 sectors, viz rag picking (63.33%), working in automobile garages, work-shops and cycle-repairing shops (13.33%), domestic service (10.00%), collection of semi-burnt coal and green coconut fibres (6.67%), potato sorting and grading (3.33%), cleaning of railway platforms and train compartments (3.33%), Tamil and Bengali each only in one sector, i.e. rag-picking (100.00%). Thus, it can be concluded that when all or most of the Bengali, Tamil, Muslim and Oriya backward caste Hindu children are engaged in the sector of rag picking, highest per cent of Schedule Caste (SC) street children are found to be engaged on the occupation of shoe-shining, repairing etc. and majority of the Scheduled Tribe (ST) Street children work as domestic servants.

In such of the specific occupations is taken into consideration a different picture comes into the sight. Interestingly collection of semi-burnt coal and green coconut fibre as a source of livelihood is confined to the Telugu children alone and the occupation of domestic service has been confined to the street children belonging to the tribal communities (62.5%).

Interestingly hotel work and collection of Potato from godown sites and confined to the Oriya backward caste Hindu children only. Specialisation of the work of potato sorting is distributed among 50 per cent of Muslim and 50 per cent of Telugu children. But the most important occupation of the street children which is found to be rag-picking has mostly been adopted by the Muslim children (35.82%). The occupation of cleaning railway platforms, train compartments and collection of tips and alms from the passengers has been adopted by only the Muslim and Telugu children with equal proportion. Surprisingly shoe-shining has been a specific job only for the Scheduled Caste children. But not a single child belonging to any other community is found to have adopted this occupation as it is considered as a derogatory and a profane job. But, even though, vending of edible items is considered prestigious, adoption of this occupation is only confined to the Oriya backward caste Hindu children.

Duration of doing the Present Job

A perusal of Table No. 4.16 makes it visible that most of the street children (30.83%) have been practicing their present jobs since lest 1-2 years. They are followed by 30 per cent of children who have been earning their livelihood for the last 3-4 years and 23.33 per cent are found to earn their livelihood since last 5-6 years. A total number of 17 children accounting for 14.67 per cent are there who had taken up their present jobs sometime/before 7-8 years and are found to still continue the same. The rest 2 (1.67%) children have been concentrating on their present jobs for last 9 years or more.

Factors Responsible for taking to the Present Occupation

The factors that have made the street children to adopt the present occupations are found to be as many 10 different reasons. In most of the cases (77.5%) the street children say that they have adopted their present occupations as per the opinion, suggestion or instruction of their parents followed by a total number of 35 children, about 29 per cent, who say that they have taken to different jobs because more of their peers are engaged in such activities. Interestingly, 20 per cent of them opine that their present jobs are more profitable than other jobs. As a result of this, they have retained the same occupations. About 12 per cent state that they happened to take up the present jobs as their brothers and sisters are also engaged in such activities. Among the rest 5 reasons, each one comprises below 10 per cent of the total sample. In descending order of importance these are: poverty or forced circumstances (9.17%), less hazardous and involvement of less risk (9.17%), tradition (6.67%), opinion or suggestion of relatives (2.50%) and death of parents; father or mother or both (2.50%).

Working Hours

In order to stay alive, each moment is challenging for the street children. 'Struggle for survival' rings as an alarm at the dawn of the morning to remind them for searching of their own food. As a result they wake up early in the morning, no matter whether they clean their face or teeth and rush to the streets of the city to earn their daily bread. Throughout the day they are to remain on streets and work hard. Otherwise they remain starved.

A perusal of Table No. 4.18 reveals that maximum street children (34.17%) remain on streets for about 9-10 hours per day followed by 24.17 per cent remaining for 7-8 hours and 11.67 per cent for 5-6 hours. An equal percentage of them are compelled to work on the streets for about 11-12 hours per day. The situation of 12 street children, 10 per cent of the total sample, is found to be horrible who work for 13 or more hours per day on the streets. But unfortunately 8.33 per cent of these children are found to be in a little better position who work only for about 2-4 hours a day. When one looks at certain occupations, with regard to utilisation of average time, it is observed that the street children who work in different hotels toil for longer duration per day that comes to be 14 hours on an average, and it is least, i.e. 3.5 hours per day in case of those who are engaged in collection of semi-burnt coal and green coconut fibres. Amongst the rest, the street children who clean railway platforms, train compartments and collect tips or alms, work for about 13 hours a day, followed by garage boys and assistants in cycle repairing shops (12.86 hours), vendors (10.5 hours), rag-pickers (9.57 hours), shoe-shiners (9.05 hours), potato collectors (7.93

hours), potato sorters (6.5 hours) and domestic servants (4.55 hours). The average working hour of the street children irrespective of occupations comes to be 9.12 hours per day (Table: 4.19).

Occupation Prior to the Present Job

So far as the occupational mobility among the street children is concerned, of the total sample as many as 38 persons, about 32 per cent, have left their earlier jobs and have taken to their present occupations. The rest (68.33%) are found to have trained their first jobs.

If the street children who had some other occupations than their present ones is consider as 100 per cent, it is found that 57.89 per cent of children were students, 10.53 per cent were sorting out potato at potato godowns and shops, 7.89 per cent were following beggary and 5.26 per cent were working as domestic servants. A total number of 2 or 5.26 per cent of them were working in transport vehicles as passenger facilitators. An equal percentage of them were working as wage-earners and about 3 percentage of them were working in motor garages, hotels, etc. (Table: 4.20).

Subsidiary Occupations

Compared to the above discussions, data presented in Table No. 4.21 represent that apart from the present occupations, a total number of 9 (7.5%) of them extract little more income from some subsidiary sources, like beggary (66.67%), rag-picking (22.22%), and wage-earning (11.11%) and as such supplement their main income earned out of their primary occupations. The rest children (92.50%), however, earn their livelihood out of only one source, i.e. their respective current occupations and try to manage themselves and satisfy their parents with the earnings from those sources.

Age at Entry into the First Job

A child is expected to start his/her formal education at the age of above 6 years but because of utter poverty, street children have been deprived of this facility. When they should attend school, they are found to be struggling for their survival on the streets. A perusal of Table No. 4.22 reveals the fact that most of the street children (48.33%) have started earning their livelihood on streets at the age of above 7-8 years. Surprisingly some 46 of them, little more than 38 per cent, have entered into such activities right from their school-going age, i.e. 5-6 years. Thus the children in the age group of 5-8 years consisting about 87 per cent of the total sample have lost the right to enjoy their childhood and availing regular or formal school curriculum.

Income and Expenditure

Table No. 4.23 represents data on weekly income of the street children according to their respective occupations. It seems that majority, i.e. 36.67 per cent of children earn in between Rs. 101/- to Rs. 200/- per week followed by 30 per cent whose income is found to be limited to Rs. 100/- or less. There are 25 (28.83%) street children, who are able to earn in between Rs. 201/- to Rs. 300/- per week. Hence the income about 88 per cent of them rests round these 3 income groups and the rest 12 per cent, however, earn more than Rs. 300/- per week. A cursory look at the same table further reveals some interesting facts. If the total sample falling in each occupational category is taken as 100 per cent and a cut off line is drawn in between the income groups of Rs. 101/- to Rs. 200/- and Rs. 201/- to Rs. 300/-, more than 60 per cent of street children having the occupation of potato collection and shoe-shining, earn some Rs. 201/- and more per week. Basing on this data, it can tentatively be said that their annual income would cross the poverty line which is fixed at Rs. 11,000/- per year and hence, as compared to others, the per capita per week income of these children belonging to these two occupational categories are found to be highest in the ascending order, i.e. Rs. 218.11 for those who collect potato and sell it in the local markets and Rs. 387.20 for the shoe-shiners. Rag-picking has been found as the most important occupation amongst the street children. But this occupation feeds only Rs. 171.43 as the per capita per week income for a child having this occupation as a source of his/her livelihood (Table: 4.21).

Collection of data on income for last 7 working days of the street children on the basis of verbal discussion with them at their working places on road would bring some inaccuracy and erroneous conclusions. Therefore, an attempt has been made to work out the per capita per day income of these children according to their respective occupations and average time spent on last working day because of the fact that it would be in their fresh memory. In this respect Table No. 4.25 shows that the per capita income of the street children irrespective of their occupations comes to be Rs. 22.93 which is much lower than the government prescribed daily (8 hours) wage of Rs. 30/- for unskilled labours (Appendix: 5). But surprisingly amongst all the street children, a hotel boy works for longest duration, i.e. about 14 hours per day on an average but earns only Rs. 28.21. On the other hand a vendor works for about 10 hours a day and his/her income exceeds Rs. 40/- (Rs. 41.25), which is much higher than the income of other street children. Further, if we look at the above table again, it reveals that among the most easily accessible jobs, like collection of semi-burnt coal and green coconut bifres, domestic service, potato collection, potato sorting, rag-picking, cleaning of railway platforms and train compartments etc. that do not require any skill or capital investment but require much physical labour, do not fetch much for the street children who have adopted such occupations. Unfortunately, the condition of those who are engaged in collection of semi-burnt coal and green coconut fibres, potato sorting and cleaning of railway platforms and train compartments are very pitiable. Their earnings come to be only Rs. 3.25, Rs. 7.00 and Rs. 8.00 respectively per day. With this meager and paltry-some income these street children are to satisfy both themselves as well as their needy family members. The per capita per day income of other street children are however, little satisfactory. It comes to be Rs. 10.26 for domestic servants, Rs. 12.43 for garage workers and those who work in cycle repairing shops, Rs. 27.21 for potato collectors, Rs. 22.79 for rag-pickers and Rs. 38.80 for the shoe-shiners.

Expenditure Pattern

It is mandatory but illogical that the children who work hard on the streets for the whole day, should hand over their whole income to their parents. But in order to stay in the family and get parental affection most of them hand over their total earning to their parents. The present study finds that 60 per cent street children have handed over their whole income of the last 7 working days to their parents followed by 32.50 per cent of them who have partly given their earning to their respective parents. A total number of 9 street children, accounting for 7.50 per cent, are found not to have given anything to their parents. This section of street children, however, have left their homes or have not kept any contact with the parents. (Table: 4.26). As a whole, it is found from Table No. 4.27 that of all the street children who have shared either the whole of their earning or part of it with their parents, have given more than 80 per cent (81.12%) of their total income on an average of the last 7 working days and kept the rest with self for consumption of edible items, narcotics or for visiting cinemas or for some other purpose.

Nature and Ways of Saving

Many street children work for prolonged hours and earn very meager amount. This does not permit them to save much or develop the habit of saving for future. However, of the total sample, 26.67 per cent of children have saved at least some of their earnings (Table 4.28) during the last 7 working days, but the per capita saving per week amongst these children comes to be only Rs. 22/- (Table 4.29). This approximately works out to be only Rs. 3/- per day per child. However, as observed during the field work, mainly the shoe shiners and Muslim rag-pickers have the habit of saving. Generally these children save their earning mostly in sealed or in earthen container (*Kumpi/ Sara*) under the custody of their mothers. Interestingly more than 84 per cent of them are found to have saved some of their earnings in earthern containers, but 12.50 per cent of them have kept their savings with their mothers. They do not have any earthen pot or any other such material to keep their savings. Surprisingly there is only 1 (3.31%) child who has left home and stays at the railway platform. He keeps his savings with his friend and so far his friend has not created any problem (Table: 4.30) for him.

Table—4.1: Distribution of street children according to residence of their parents/guardians

Type/place of residence	*Total cases*	*% age*
Abandoned/semi constructed building	12	10.00
Basti/village	106	88.3
Pavement	1	0.83
Railway platform	1	0.83
Total	**120**	**100.00**

Table—4.2: Category of street children according to family contracts

Category	*Total cases*	*% age*
Children on the street	106	88.33
Children of the street	12	10.00
Abandoned/orphan/neglected children	2	1.67
Total	**120**	**100.00**

Table—4.3: Distribution of street children according to age and sex

Age group (in years)	*Boys*	*Girls*	*Total*
7-8	10 (11.11)	6 (20.00)	16 (13.33)
9-10	22 (24.44)	11 (36.67)	33 (27.50)
11-12	23 (25.56)	6 (20.00)	29 (24.17)
13-14	35 (38.89)	7 (23.33)	42 (35.00)
Total	**90 (100.00)**	**30 (100.00)**	**120 (100.00)**

Note: Figures in brackets represent % age.

Table—4.4: Distribution of the street children according to place of birth

Place	*Total cases*	*% age*
Bhubaneswar city	42	35.00
Other than Bhubaneswar city	74	61.67
Do not know/no answer	4	3.33
Total	**120**	**100.00**

Table—4.5: Distribution of the street children according to religion

Religion	*Total cases*	*% age*
Animism	8	6.67
Hindu	85	70.83
Muslim	27	22.50
Total	**120**	**100.00**

Table—4.6: Distribution of street children according to linguistic community

Linguistic community	*Total cases*	*% age*
Bengali	1	0.83
Urdu (Muslim)	27	22.50
Oriya (caste Hindu)	38	31.67
Scheduled caste (Oriya/Telugu)	13	10.83
Scheduled tribe	8	6.67
Tamil	3	2.50
Telugu	30	25.00
Total	**120**	**100.00**

Table—4.7: Distribution of street children according to caste/tribe

Caste/Tribe	*Total cases*	*% age*
Barika (Barber)	2	1.67
Chasa/Khandayat (Agriculturist/warrior)	2	1.67
Gauda (Cattle Herder)	6	5.00
Kumbhara (Potters)	1	0.83
Matia (Earth cutter)	11	9.17
Mochi (Cobbler)	10	8.33
Sabara (Tribal)	8	6.67
Tanti (Weaver)	1	0.83
Do not know/No answer	79	65.83
Total	**120**	**100.00**

Table—4.8: Living parents (father/mother) of the street children

Variables	*Total cases*	*% age*
Fathers not alive	10	8.33
Mothers not alive	7	5.83
Both not alive	1	0.83
Both alive	102	85.00
Total	**120**	**100.00**

Table—4.9: Shelter of Street Children

Shelter	*Total cases*	*% age*
Abandoned/dilapidated house	2	1.67
Garage/hotel premise	2	1.67
Railway platform	7	5.83
Market complex premise	2	1.67
Relative's house	1	0.83
With parents at home	106	88.33
Total	**120**	**100.00**

Table—4.10: Years of staying outside home among 'children of street' and abandoned/orphan/neglected children

Duration (in years)	*Total cases*	*% age*
<1	3	21.43
1-2	5	35.71
3+	6	42.86
Total	**14**	**100.00**

Table—4.11: Factors responsible for staying outside home among 'children of street' and abandoned/orphan/neglected children (N = 14)

Sl. No.	*Factors*	*Total cases*	*% age*
1.	Broken family	4	28.57
2.	Death of parents (Mother/Father/Both)	2	14.29
3.	Lack of space at Home and self decision to spend night at other place	2	14.29
4.	Late night working pattern	2	14.29
5.	More income facility at railway station	3	21.43
6.	Out of anguish/suffering torture/regular conflict with parents	9	64.29

Table—4.12: Educational status among street children

Level of education	*Total cases*	*% age*
Illiterate	93	77.50
Primary (I-V)	24	20.00
Middle (VI-VII)	2	167
Upto high school but below matriculation	1	0.83
Total	**120**	**100.00**

Table—4.13: Street children presently continuing formal and non-formal education (NFE)

Type of education	*Total cases*	*% age*
Formal	5	4.17
Non-formal	26	21.67
Dropout/not continuing formal/ non-formal education/others	84	70.00
Total	**120**	**100.00**

Table—4.14: Distribution of street children according to sex and occupation

Sl. No.	*Occupation*	*Boys*	*Girls*	*Total*
1.	Collection of semi-burnt coal and green coconut fibre		2 (6.67)	2 (6.67)
2.	Domestic service	1 (1.11)	9 (30.00)	10 (8.33)
3.	Garage work/asst. at cycle repairing shop	7 (7.78)	–	7 (5.83)
4.	Hotel work	2 (2.22)	–	2 (1.67)
5.	Potato collection	12 (13.33)	2 (6.67)	14 (11.67)
6.	Potato sorting	1 (1.11)	1 (1.33)	2 (1.67)
7.	Rag-picking	52 (57.78)	15 (50.00)	67 (55.83)
8.	Railway platform and train compartment cleaning and collection tips and alms	2 (2.22)	–	2 (1.67)
9.	Shoe-shining	10 (11.11)	–	10 (8.33)
10.	Vending	3 (3.33)	1 (1.33)	4 (3.33)
	Total	**90 (100.00)**	**30 (100.00)**	**120 (100.00)**

Table—4.15: Occupation of street children according to linguistic communities

Linguistic minority community	Occupation										
	Collection of semi-burnt coal and green coconut fibre	*Domestic service*	*Garage Boy/asst. at cycle repairing shop*	*Hotel asst.*	*Potato collection*	*Potato sorting*	*Rag picking*	*Railway platform and train compartment cleaning and collection of tips and alms*	*Shoe shining*	*Vending*	*Total*
(1)	*(2)*	*(3)*	*(4)*	*(5)*	*(6)*	*(7)*	*(8)*	*(9)*	*(10)*	*(11)*	*(12)*
ST		5 (62.5) [50.00]					3 (37.5) [4.48]				8 (100.00) [6.67]
Oriya (SC)							3 (23.08) [4.48]		10 (76.92) [100.00]		13 (100.00) [10.53]
Oriya (Caste Hindu)		2 (5.26) [20.00]	2 (5.26) [28.57]	2 (5.26) [100.00]	14 (36.84) [100.00]		14 (36.84) [10.91]			4 (10.53) [100.00]	38 (100.00) [31.67]
Urdu (Muslim)			1 (3.7) [14.29]			1 (3.7) [50.00]	24 (88.89) [35.82]	1 (3.33) [50.00]			27 (10.00) [22.5]

(Contd...)

(1)	(2)	(3)	(4)	(5)	(6)	(7)	(8)	(9)	(10)	(11)	(12)
Telegu	2 (6.67) [100.00]	3 (10.00) [30.00]	4 (13.33) [57.14]			1 (3.33) [50.00]	19 (63.33) [25.26]	1 (3.33) [50.00]			30 (100.00) [25.00]
Tamil							3 (100.00) [4.48]				3 (100.00) [2.5]
Bengali							1 (100.00) [1.49]				1 (100.00) [0.83]
Total	**2 (1.67) [100.00]**	**10 (8.33) [100.00]**	**7 (5.83) [100.00]**	**2 (1.67) [100.00]**	**14 (11.67) [100.00]**	**2 (1.67) [10.00]**	**67 (55.53) [100.00]**	**2 (1.67) [100.00]**	**10 (6.33) [100.00]**	**4 (3.33) [100.00]**	**120 (100.00) [100.00]**

Note: Figures in '()' indicates % age to total sample of each community and figures in '[ ]' indicates % age to each occupation.

Table—4.16: Duration of practicing present occupations among street children

Duration (in year)	Total cases	% age
1-2	37	30.83
3-4	36	30.00
5-6	28	23.33
7-8	17	14.67
9 and more	2	1.67
Total	**120**	**100.00**

Table—4.17: Factors responsible for taking to the present occupations (N = 120)

Sl. No.	Factors	Total cases	% age
1.	As per the opinion/suggestion/instruction of parents	93	77.5
2.	As per the opinion/suggestion of relatives	3	2.50
3.	As more peers are engaged in this work	35	29.17
4.	As brother(s)/sisters(s) are engaged in this work	14	11.67
5.	As it is more profitable	24	20.00
6.	As it is less hazardous and involves less risk	11	9.17
7.	Death of parents	3	2.50
8.	Poverty/forced by circumstances	11	9.17
9.	Traditional occupation	8	6.67
10.	Decision by self to raise own money to spend independently	12	10.00

Table—4.18: Working hours of the street children per day

Duration of work (in hours)	Total cases	% age
2-4	10	8.33
5-6	14	11.67
7-8	29	24.17
9-10	41	34.17
11-12	14	11.67
13 and more	12	10.00
Total	**120**	**100.00**

Table—4.19: Average working hour per day according to occupations

Sl. No.	Occupations	Total persons engaged	Total time spend in last working day (in hours)	Average
1.	Collection of semi-burnt coal and collection of green coconut fibre	2	7	3.5
2.	Domestic service	10	45.5	4.55
3.	Garage boy/Asst at cycle repairing shop	7	90	12.86
4.	Hotel assistant	2	28	14.00
5.	Potato collection	14	111	7.93
6.	Potato sorting	2	13	6.5
7.	Rag-picking	67	641.5	9.57
8.	Railway platform and train compartment cleaning	2	26	13.00
9.	Shoe-shining	10	90.5	9.05
10.	Vending	4	42	10.5
	Total	**120**	**1094.5**	**9.12**

Table—4.20: Occupation of the street children prior to the present job

Sl. No.	Occupation	Total cases	% age
1.	Beggary	3	2.5 (7.89)
2.	Domestic service	2	1.67 (5.26)
3.	Garage boy	1	0.83 (2.63)
4.	Helper in Butchers shop	1	0.83 (2.63)
5.	Helper in motor vehicles	2	1.67 (5.26)
6.	Hotel boy	1	0.83 (2.63)
7.	Potato sorting	4	3.33 (10.53)
8.	Student	22	18.33 (57.89)
9.	Wage-earning	2	1.67 (5.26)
	Sub-total	38	31.67(100.00)
	Nil	82	68.33
	Total	**120**	**100.00**

Note: Figures in brackets represent % age to the sub-total.

Table—4.21: Age of the street children at entry into the first Job

Age group	*Total cases*	*% age*
5-6	46	38.33
7-8	58	48.33
9-10	9	7.5
11-12	5	4.17
13-14	2	1.67
Total	**120**	**120.00**

Table—4.22: Subsidiary occupation Among the Street Children

Occupation	*Total cases*	*% age*
Beggary	6	5.00 (66.67)
Rig-picking	2	1.67 (22.22)
Wage-earning	1	0.83 (11.11)
Sub-total	9	7.50 (100.00)
Nil	111	92.50
Total	**120**	**100.00**

Table—4.23: Weekly income of street children according to occupation and income ranges

Sl. No.	Occupation	Total sample	Range of income (in Rs.)						Remarks
			<100	101-200	201-300	301-400	401-500	501 +	
1.	Collection of semi-burnt coal and green coconut fibre	2 (100.00)	2 (100.00)	–	–	–	–	–	
2.	Domestic service	10 (100.00)	9 (90.00)	1 (10.00)	–	–	–	–	
3.	Garage work/Asst. at cycle repairing shop	7 (100.00)	4 (57.14)	1 (14.29)	2 (25.57)	–	–	–	
4.	Hotel work	2 (100.00)	–	–	–	2 (100.00)	–	–	
5.	Potato collection	14 (100.00)	2 (14.29)	3 (21.43)	5 (35.71)	3 (21.43)	1 (7.14)	–	
6.	Potato sorting	2 (100.00)	2 (100.00)	–	–	–	–	–	
7.	Rag picking	67 (100.00)	13 (19.40)	37 (55.22)	14 (20.90)	3 (4.48)	–	–	
8.	Railway platform and train compartment cleaning and collecting tips and alm	2 (100.00)	2 (100.00)	–	–	–	–	–	
9.	Shoe shining	10 (100.00)	1 (10.00)	1 (10.00)	2 (20.00)	4 (40.00)	2 (20.00)	–	
10.	Vending	4 (100.00)	1 (25.00)	1 (25.00)	2 (50.00)	–	–	–	
	Total	**120.00 (100.00)**	**36 (30.00)**	**44 (36.67)**	**25 (20.83)**	**5 (6.67)**	**5 (4.17)**	**2 (1.67)**	

Note: Food assistance which is received as alms by the domestic servants from their employees has not been taken into consideration.

Table—4.24: Per capita weekly i..come of the street children according to occupations

Sl. No.	*Occupation*	*Total sample*	*Total income*	*Per capita per week*
1.	Collection of semi-burnt coal and green coconut fibre	2	100.80	50.40
2.	Domestic service	10	620.00	62.00
3.	Garage work/Asst. at cycle repairing shop	7	601.00	85.86
4.	Hotel work	2	395.00	197.50
5.	Potato collection	14	3053.50	218.11
6.	Potato sorting	2	185.00	92.50
7.	Rag-picking	67	11,485.90	171.43
8.	Railway platform and train compartment cleaning and collection tips and alms	2	128.90	64.45
9.	Shoe-shining	10	3872.00	387.2
10.	Vending	4	859.00	214.75
	Total	**120**	**20733.10**	**172.78**

Note: As per table no. 4.23.

Table—4.25: Per capita daily income of street children according occupation and average working hour per day

Sl. No.	*Occupation*	*Total sample*	*Average working hour per person per day*	*Total income earned per day (last day) (in R)*	*Per capita per day*
(1)	*(2)*	*(3)*	*(4)*	*(5)*	*(6)*
1.	Collection of semi-burnt coal and green coconut fibres	2	3.5	6.50	3.25
2.	Domestic service	10	4.55	102.60	10.26
3.	Garage work/Asst. at cycle repairing shop	7	12.86	87.00	12.43
4.	Hotel work	2	14.00	56.43	28.21
5.	Potato collection	14	7.93	389.00	27.79

(Contd...)

(1)	(2)	(3)	(4)	(5)	(6)
6.	Potato-sorting	2	6.50	14.00	7.00
7.	Rag-picking	67	9.57	1526.85	22.79
8.	Railway platform, train compartment cleaning and collection tips and alms	2	13.00	16.00	8.00
9.	Shoe-shining	10	9.05	388.00	38.80
10.	Vending	4	10.5	165.00	41.25
	Total	**120**	**9.12**	**2751.38**	**22.93**

Table—4.26: Expenditure pattern among the street children (last 7 working days)

Variables	*Total cases*	*% age*
Whole income given to parents	72	60.00
Part of income given to parents	39	32.50
Not given any income to parents	9	7.50
Total	**120**	**100.00**

Table—4.27: Expenditure Pattern Among Street Children According to Occupation-wise Income

Sl. No.	*Occupation*	*Total sample*	*Total income earned last week*	*Amount given to parents*	*Amount kept with self*
(1)	(2)	(3)	(4)	(5)	(6)
1.	Collection of semi-burnt coal and green coconut fibre	2	100.80	100.80	
2.	Domestic service	10	620.00	508.00	112.00
3.	Garage work/asst. at cycle repairing shop	7	258.00 (100.00)	87 (33.72)	171.00 (66.28)
4.	Hotel work	2	170.00 (100.00)	110 (64.21)	60.00 (35.29)
5.	Potato collection	14	3053.50 (100.00)	3053.50 (100.00)	-
6.	Potato sorting	2	185.00 (100.00)	125.00 (67.57)	50.00 (32.43)

(Contd...)

(1)	(2)	(3)	(4)	(5)	(6)
7.	Rag-picking	67	11,485.90 (100.00)	10,113.90 (48.48)	1372.00 (51.52)
8.	Railway platforms, train compartment cleaning and collecting tips and alms	2	128.90 (100.00)	24.00 (18.62)	104.90 (81.38)
9.	Shoe-shining	10	3872.00 (100.00)	1877.00 (48.48)	1995.00 (51.52)
10.	Vending	4	859.00 (100.00)	820.00 (95.46)	39.00 (4.54)
	Total	**120**	**20733.10** **(100.00)**	**16819.20** **(81.12)**	**3913.90** **(18.18)**

Note: Figures in brackets represent % age.

Table—4.28: Nature of savings among street children (last week)

Variables	*Total cases*	*% age*
Saving	32	26.67
Not saving	88	73.33
Total	**120**	**100.00**

Table—4.29: Per capita savings per week among street children

Range (in Rs.)	*Total cases*	*Total money saved in last week*	*Average per child per week*
1-10	10	65.50	6.55
11-20	7	96.00	13.71
21-30	6	148.00	24.67
31 +	9	391.00	43.44
Total	**32**	**700.50**	**21.89**

Table—4.30: Ways of saving among street children

Variables	*Total cases*	*% age*
Earthern savings pot	27	84.38
With mother	4	12.50
With friend	1	3.13
Total	**32**	**100.00**

5

Struggle for Survival

The Problems of Street Children

Illiteracy, over population, poverty and the problem of unemployment among a large chuck of traditional Indian population propel to leave thousands of innocent children into the streets of developing urban centres. Thus, the street children, can, in one way be treated as the by-product of these negative issues which stand against maintenance of good quality of life (Q.O.L).

Occupational Hazards

Deterioration of quality of life (Q.O.L) starts soon after the poor immigrants in urban centres are maladjusted and their subjunctive hopes become futile. In this context when we discuss the present familial problems of the street children in Bhubaneswar city, it seems that both the parents as well as children struggle for their survival and try to enhance their quality of life (Q.O.L). But high rate of illiteracy among the parents of these children (Table 3.4) has necessitated them to adopt a number of low income generating occupations (4.14) in order to sustain their life and to economically support their families which constitute a large number of members per family (Table 3.3). This leads to disorganisation of familial tie between parents and children. In many cases (75.00%) parents become addicted to alcoholic drinks (Table 5.1) in order to get rid of hypertension, bodily pain and psycho-economic pressure of supporting their large familial dependents with their meager daily income in a maladjusted socio-culture-ecological niche. Apart from this, parents (19.01%) also suffer from various diseases (Table 5.2), the most important ones being viral fever (33.33%) colic or abdominal pain (23.8%) etc. (Table 5.3) compel them to ask their children to work for themselves as well as for their parents and other family members. Relating to this, as many as 87 (82.08%) children belonging to the first category of children, i.e. 'children on street' say that they are asked by their parents to work and earn daily (Table 5.4). Not only they are simply asked to work and earn daily rather in case of 27.59 per cent of children some large amount of target is fixed up by their parents for earning daily (Table 5.5) which, in most of the cases (37.50%) comes to be Rs. 10/- per day followed by 29.17 per cent of children for whom it is as high as Rs. 30/- per day and in case of 20.83 per cent street children the target amount fixed for earning daily is in between Rs. 21/- and Rs. 30/- (Table 5.6). When they do not work as per the advice of their parents and earn accordingly, they are scolded and are also beaten up (89.53%). At times they are not given adequate food (30.23%), and even in many cases (20.93%) food is completely denied. For about 7 per cent of children, their parents close the doors and in such cases the children become disappointed and helpless (Table 5.7). Because of these embarrassing situation, about 18 per cent of the total children (Table 5.8) did not come to their respective homes atleast for once during the last week out of fear of being scolded or beaten up when they had not worked so as to meet the demands of their parents. In this regard Table No. 5.9 illustrates that of the total 19 children, about 74 per cent of them had not come to their respective homes for about 1-2 days during the last week and they had spent their nights mostly at the railway platforms (73.68%), market complex premises (15.79%), community halls or meeting-pendals of their bastes (5.26%) etc. (Table 5.10).

Use of Earnings of the Street Children by their Parents

It was said in the last chapter that most of the street children (about 90.1%) give a large share of their daily earnings to their parents. When a question on the ways of spending of their earning by their respective parents was asked, 97.17 per cent of them opined that their parents spend it for the general purpose of family. But 34.91 per cent of them claim that most often their fathers take it for consumption of alcohol followed by 29.25 per cent who said that at times their fathers do so, but for most of the times their money is spent for the general management of the family. About 2 per cent of girl children opined that their earnings are mostly saved for the purpose of their marriages. In one case a girl child said that her earning is regularly sent to her village for the education of her brothers and in the rest one case, the income is adjusted towards his lodging and boarding at his relative's (Father's sister's) house where he has been staying for last two years after the death of his father and thereafter development of madness of his mother (Table 5.11).

Nourishment and Addiction

Food or nutritional intake is one of the three basic needs of life. But it is the most important requirement for sustenance of life and hence it has direct linkage with physical and mental growth and also development of working ability of a person. If a child takes required amount of food according to its age and bodily growth, it grows properly and works accordingly. But the poor economic condition of the parents of a number of street children does not permit them to feed their children properly. On the other hand their poor economic condition compels the children to work hard and earn daily. At times some of the children remain unfed and often they remain underfed. Subsequently they become malnourished. Still then, repeatedly they fight against it to work hard and earn daily.

A perusal of Table 5.12 throws some light on the dieting pattern of the street children for the day before the interview was conducted. It is found that 13.33 per cent of children had not taken any breakfast before they went to the streets for earning their days bread. Surprisingly 1.67 per cent of them had no other way than to spend the whole day without a lunch. Further 4.17 per cent of them could not have dinner before they went to sleep. In between the time of lunch and dinner, only about 56 per cent had some tiffins and the rest remained hungry. When about 49 per cent had adequate breakfast, the rest were underfed. Still about 72 per cent were satisfied with lunch against 75 per cent who had dinner to their hearts content. Tiffins were adequately available for only 69 per cent of these children (Table 5.13). Hence as we see that quite a sizable number of these children remained underfed, they are starved. But still then they were not relieved from working daily on the streets.

Intoxication of various drugs, sometimes proves to be as a social medicine which temporarily helps to resist hunger and empowers to work more. It has however bad effects on health condition of the addicts. As a result, addictive behaviour of these children reflects some amazing findings. Table No. 5.14 explains that little less than 50 per cent of these children are addicted to various intoxicants, like betel (60.34%), *bidi* or cigar (24.14%), *khaini* or tobacco (27.59%), alcoholic drinks (12.07%) and ordinary betel *masala* (10.34%). Hence, highest percentage of these children are found to have been addicted to betel leaf (Table 5.15).

Health and Hygienic Condition

Since most of the street children live in unhygienic environments, remain underfed and work hard in empty stomach they suffer miserably from various ailments and diseases. It is found from the Table No. 5.16 that one-fourths of the street children are presently suffering from many diseases, like scabies (30.00%), wounds on feet and body (26.67%), cold and cough (23.33%), joint pain (20.00%), mild fever (10.00%), itching on feet and hand (6.67%) headache (3.33%), dog-bite (3.33%), polio (3.33%), and tuberculosis (3.33%) etc. (Table 5.17).

These findings otherwise signify that working in unhygienic conditions and neglecting personal hygienic care cause scribes to a large number of street children, cold and cough affects a sizeable children as they remain exposed to sun, rain and cold (Table 5.26) for a major part of time, joint-pain is very obvious for them as each child is to cover a long distance by walk on every working day. Suffering from itching is a problem mainly with the girl street children who usually work as maid-servants and are supposed to do such works like cleaning of utensils, house floors, washing clothes etc. Even though, these children suffer from these diseases, they (73.33%) do not take any remedial measure unless they become very serious. A total number of 4 (13.33%) diseased children are, however, found to have consulted doctors and local health workers as against 6.67 per cent who have just consulted the salesmen of medicine shops and purchased medicines as per their prescriptions to avoid consultation fee with a doctor and also to save time. There are an equal percentage of these children whose parents are taking care to cure them through the local traditional healers (Table 5.18).

So far as the diseases from which the street children have ever suffered during the last two years are concerned, Table No. 5.19 and Table 5.20 illustrate some striking features. The former table shows that of the total sample of 120 street children as many as 92 (76.67%) of them have suffered from diseases atleast once during the last two years. But the latter, table focuses about the major diseases which have occurred among these children. These are found to be viral fever (42.39%), scabies (36.00%), cold and cough (31.52%), mild fever (19.57%), diarrhoea (17.39%), wounds (10.87%), malaria (9.78%), joint-pain (8.70%), headache (4.35%), abdominal-pain (3.26%), vomiting (4.76%), blister (2.20%), carbuncle (2.20%), jaundice (1.09%), polio (1.09%) and tuberculosis (1.09%).

Taking care of personal hygiene is very important to keep oneself healthy, jovial and energetic. But the hygienic awareness among the street children is very poor. As a result 29.17 per cent of them do not clean their teeth regularly (Table 5.21). To a question relating to the frequency of days the irregular street children have not cleaned their teeth in the last week, 50 per cent or 18 children are found not to have cleaned their teeth for 1 to 2 days followed by 31.43 per cent or 11 children who have neglected this personal hygienic care for 3 to 4 days. Surprisingly there are as many as 14.29 per cent or 5 children who are found to have been very irregular to take care of their teeth by daily brushing. These children have not cleaned their teeth for 5-6 days. The rest one (2.86%) child has not cleaned its teeth even for a single day during the last week (Table 5.22).

The street children roam here and there throughout the day around their working sites and their body collects a variables of uncountable dirty particles and germs which necessitate them to clean their body by regular bath. But only about 61 per cent of them are found to have taken bath regularly for the last 7 days (interview conducted in between 18th January to 5th February). The rest 39 per cent are found to be irregular in taking bath as this period was relatively cold (Table 5.23). Regarding the number of days they have not taken bath during last 7 days, 26 cent say that they had not taken bath for 1-2 days, followed by 19.15 per cent who had stopped taking bath for 3-4 days. Little more than 3 per cent are found to have not taken bath for as many 5-6 days during the lapse of last 7 days. And the rest one (1.06%) child has not taken bath even for a single day within the said period (Table 5.24).

Since the street children are exposed to many unclean jobs, they must be very cautious to keep up their nails short and clean these regularly otherwise germs pass on to food materials and enter into their body. It creates various deadly diseases, like diarrhoea, malaria, vomiting etc. But fortunately the occupations of the street children normally do not permit them to have long nails. Still, even though most of these children have short nails, these are not found to be clean in case of as many as 79 or 65.83 per cent of children. On the countary there are 26 (21.67%) children who have long and unclean nails. Not a single child is found to have long and clean nails against 12.5 per cent who have, however, maintained their nails shorts and clean (Table 5.28).

Clothing is considered as one of the basic necessities of life. But all the street children do not even possess the minimum required clothing, like pant, shirt, winter dress, foot-wear etc. Table No. 5.26 illustrates that there are 1.67 per cent of children who do not have any pant as against 6.67 per cent who are lacking even a single shirt to cover up their body. In winter season the condition of these children become very miserable as 90 per cent of them do not possess any winter garment and hence are exposed to cold. As a result while working on streets in winter, most of them catch cold and cough. Possession of foot wears is limited only to 65 per cent of these children but the rest are to work on bare foot (Table 5.26).

Regarding the number of possession of the above dress materials and foot wears, Table No. 5.27 shows that most, i.e. 57.67 per cent possess 1-2 pants as against 44.44 per cent who own shirts in this range. But since all the boy street children do not have pant or shirts, 38 or 55.88 per cent of them exchange their dresses with their younger or elder brothers whenever possible. There are 16 girl street children in total who have younger or elder sisters with whom they can exchange their dress materials, and all of them practise exchanging of one another's dress depending upon their needs (Table 5.28).

Washing of dress materials is very important and essential to avoid skin diseases and also to look pleasant. But the observation made on the day of the survey indicates that cleanliness of garments of the street children is very poor in most (42.50%) of the cases followed by 38.33 per cent of children whose dresses are rated as very unclean. In case of about 12 per cent of children, their wearings look unclean but the rest 7.5 per cent of children however, wear clean dresses (Table 5.29).

Present Occupation and Future Perspectives

The present study also made an enquiry about the future perspectives of the street children. The result is presented in Table No. 5.30. It indicates that maximum (40.00%) children do not think about their future and are skeptic to stick to their present jobs. They are followed by 22.50 per cent who say that they would shift from their present occupations to rickshaw and trolley pulling business in future. Little more than 18 per cent opine that they would earn their livelihood out of wage-earning. Among the others, 8.33 per cent say that they would become garage workers or mechanical assistants. Next to them, 5.83 per cent expect to undertake vending business (balloon, betel leaf cigar, fruits etc.). About 4 per cent think that they would be able to raise some capital and then take to some petty business, like, shop-keeping, tailoring, cycle repairing etc. The rest one child desperately opines that he would become a beggar in future (Table 5.30).

Subsequently a question on their present plight was asked and the responses are as follows: as many as 62.50 per cent at street children blame their fathers for their present condition followed by 20.83 per cent who opine that it is because of their poor economic condition. The other reasons which are pointed out by these children as responsible factors for their present misery are: bad luck (5.00%), heredity (3.33%), death of parents (2.50%), broken family (2.50%), influence of peers (2.50%), etc. (Table 5.31).

Educational Choice and Aspiration Level

In order to find out the interest among the street children to avail formal education if provided by government free of cost with lodging and boarding facilities, 36.67 per cent of them are found to be interested to avail of the facility (Table 5.32). But when a succeeding question was put on the subject relating what they would do after being educated, 34.09 per cent of the total interested children told that they would do some petty business (book selling, cycle shop, shoe shop, tailoring, tea shop etc.) followed by 27.27 per cent who expected employment in some technical trades, like becoming mechanical assistants and motor vehicle drivers. Little more than 9 per cent of them were found to be realistic to become teaching professionals and 6.62 per cent hoped that they would take to some salaried jobs. Among the rest, 4.55 per cent opined that they would become simply wage-earners followed by 2.27 per cent who expected that they would avail of some better job opportunities (Table 5.33).

Attitude of the Public: Security and Safety of Street Children

Attitudinal aspects of the general public, municipal officials, railway and police officers towards the street children are highlighted in Table No. 5.34. It points out that during the last year while 13.33 per cent of these children have been harassed by the general public, it is 7.5 per cent of children who were put in trouble by the railway and police officials. A total number of 4(3.33%) children say that they have been put in difficult situations by the municipal officials also.

Generally these children (rag pickers and domestic servants etc.) are often scolded and even beaten up by some public whenever there is in theft case. In many cases they are also handed over to the police even if they are not involved in such cases. In this context the case studies available in appendix 8 may be referred to. The shoe shiners who open their mobile petty shops at road sides of railway stations, are most often beaten up or their shops are thrown out by the railway police mainly during the peak business hours or during arrival of Ministers and others such VIPs. Sometimes municipal officers also create much problem for these children. When they open their mobile shops on foot-paths in the city, the municipal officials either destroy their belongings or cease those to harass them.

To a question on overall feelings of the street children on themselves, more than 50 per cent feel good about their present life. This has happened so since they are acquainted with their day-to-day problems and sufferings and find happiness within the situations. The rest children feel bad (16.67%), gloomy about their future (8.33%). The remaining 11.67 per cent children could not answer to the question (Table 3.5).

Table—5.1: Consumption of spirit/alcohol among the parents (father) of street children

Variables	*Total cases*	*% age*
Consume	83	75.00
Do not consume	27	24.55
Total	**110**	**100.00**

Table—5.2: Present health status of parents (fathers) of the street children

Variables	*Total class*	*% age*
Suffering	21	19.9
Do not suffer	89	80.91
Total	**110**	**100.00**

Table—5.3: Diseases among diseased parents of street children (N = 21)

Sl. No.	*Disease*	*Total cases*	*% age*
1.	Asthma	2	9.52
2.	Abdominal pain	5	23.80
3.	Viral fever/malaria/vomiting	7	33.33
4.	High blood pressure	1	4.76
5.	Headache	4	19.05
6.	Joint pain	4	19.05
7.	Madness	2	9.52
8.	Paralysis (Partial)	1	4.76
9.	Tuberculosis	1	4.76

Table—5.4: Whether parents ask you to do work and earn daily (among children on street)?

Responses	*Total cases*	*% age*
Yes	87	82.08
No	19	17.92
Total	100	100.00

Table—5.5: If yes, do they Fix up any target amount to earn daily?

Responses	*Total cases*	*% age*
Yes	24	27.59
No	63	72.41
Total	87	100.00

Table—5.6: Target amount fixed up for the last day

Target amount fixed (in Rs.)	*Total cases*	*% age*
1-10	7	37.5
11-20	3	12.5
21-30	5	20.83
31+	7	29.17
Total	**24**	**100.00**

Table—5.7: What happens when you do not work according to the wish of your parents (N = 86)

Variables	*Total cases*	*% age*
At times adequate food is not given	26	30.23
At times food is denied	18	20.93
At times door is closed	6	6.8
Many times scolded and beaten up	77	89.53

Table—5.8: Have you ever not returned to home out of fear last week

Responses	*Total cases*	*% age*
Yes	19	17.92
No	87	82.08
Total	**106**	**100.00**

Table—5.9: If yes, how many times last week

No. of times (in days)	*Total cases*	*% age*
1	7	36.84
2	7	36.84
3	3	15.89
4+	2	10.53
Total	**19**	**100.00**

Table—5.10: In such cases, where did you stay?

Place	*Total cases*	*% age*
Railway platform	14	73.68
Community hall/meeting pendal of basti/slum/village	1	5.26
Garage	1	5.26
Market complex premise	3	15.79
Total	**19**	**100.00**

Table—5.11: How your income is spent by your parents (N = 106)?

Responses	*Total cases*	*% age*
Spent for the general purpose of family	103	97.17
For majority of times father takes it for consumption of alcoholic drink	31	29.25
At times father takes it for consumption of alcohol	37	34.91
It is sent to village for education of brothers/sisters	1	0.94
It is saved for marriage purpose of self/sister	2	1.89
Adjusted towards food charges at relative's house	1	0.94

Table—5.12: Status of Consumption of food in last day (N = 120)

	Whether consumed			
Variables	*Yes*	*% age*	*No*	*% age*
Breakfast	101	86.67	16	13.33
Lunch	118	98.33	2	1.67
Tiffin	67	55.83	53	44.17
Dinner	115	95.83	5	4.17

Table—5.13: Quantity of consumption of food on last day (N = 120)

Variables	*No. of children consumed*	*Level of consumption*			
		Adequate	*% age*	*Inadequate*	*% age*
Breakfast	104 (100.00)	51	49.04	53	50.96
Lunch	118 (100.00)	85	72.03	33	27.97
Tiffin	67 (100.00)	42	62.69	25	37.31
Dinner	115 (100.00)	86	74.78	29	25.22

Table—5.14: Number of street children addicted to narcotics

Variables	*Total*	*%*
Addicted	58	48.33
Not addicted	62	51.67
Total	**120**	**100.00**

Table—5.15: Types of narcotics consumed among addicted street children (N = 58)

Type	*Total cases*	*% age*
Bidi/cigar	14	24.14
Khaini	16	27.59
Liquor/spirit	67	12.07
Ordinary pan masala (pudia)	6	10.34
Betel (pan)	35	60.34

Table—5.16: Number street children presently suffering from some ailments diseases

Purpose	*Total cases*	*% age*
Yes	30	25.00
No	90	75.00
Total	**120**	**100.00**

Table—5.17: Type of ailments of diseases among ailing diseased street children (N = 30)

Sl. No.	*Disease*	*Total cases*	*% age*
1.	Cold and cough	7	23.33
2.	Dog bite	1	3.33
3.	Headache	1	3.33
4.	Itching	2	6.67
5.	Joint pain	6	20.00
6.	Mild fever	3	10.00
7.	Polio	1	3.33
8.	Scabies	9	30.00
9.	Tuberculosis	1	3.33
10.	Would on feet and body	8	26.67

Table—5.18: Types of treatment going on among ailing diseased street children (N = 30)

Sl. No.	*Type of treatment*	*Total cases*	*% age*
1.	Consultation with doctor/health worker	4	13.33
2.	Consultation with sales men	2	6.67
3.	Consultation with traditional healer	2	6.67
4.	No treatment	22	73.33
	Total	**30**	**100.00**

Table—5.19: Number of street children who have suffered at least once from some disease during the last two years

Variables	*Total cases*	*% age*
Suffered at least once from some diseases	92	76.67
Not suffered from any disease	28	23.33
Total	**120**	**100.00**

Table—5.20: Name of the diseases the dtreet children have ever suffered from during the last two years (N = 92)

Sl. No.	*Disease*	*Total cases*	*% age*
1.	Abdominal pain	3	3.26
2.	Blister	2	2.2
3.	Carbuncle	2	2.2
4.	Cold and cough	29	31.52
5.	Diarrhoea	16	17.39
6.	Dig bite	1	1.09
7.	Headache	4	4.35
8.	Itching	2	2.17
9.	Jaundice	1	1.09
10.	Joint pain	8	8.70
11.	Malaria	9	9.78
12.	Mild fever	18	19.57
13.	Polio	1	1.09
14.	Scabies	34	36.00
15.	Tuberculosis	1	1.09
16.	Viral fever	39	42.39
17.	Vomiting	3	3.26
18.	Wound	10	10.87

Table—5.21: Number of street children who clean their teeth regularly

Variable	*Total cases*	*% age*
Regular	85	70.85
Irregular	35	29.17
Total	**120**	**100.00**

Table—5.22: Number of days teeth not cleaned during last week among irregular street children

Frequency (in days)	*Total cases*	*% age*
1-2	18	51.43
3-4	110	31.43
5-6	5	14.29
7	1	2.86
Total	**35**	**100.00**

Table—5.23: Number of street children who have taken bath regularly in the last week

Variables	*Total cases*	*% age*
Regular	73	60.83
Irregular	47	39.17
Total	**120**	**100.00**

Note: Interview held between 18 January to 3rd February.

Table—5.24: Number of days bath not taken during last week among irregular street children

Frequency (in days)	*Total cases*	*% age*
1-2	25	26.50
3-4	18	19.15
5-6	3	3.19
7	1	1.06
Total	**47**	**100.00**

Note: As per Table No. 5.19.

Table—5.25: Status of nail among street children

Status of Nail	*Total cases*	*% age*
Short and clean	15	12.5
Short and unclean	79	65.83
Long and clean	–	–
Long and unclean	26	21.67
Total	**120**	**100.00**

Table—5.26: Possession of clothing and foot wears among street children (N = 120)

Clothing/foot wear	*Possess*	*Do not possess*
Pant	118 (98.33)	2 (1.67)
Shirt/T-shirt	108 (90.00)	8 (6.67)
Winter garments	12 (10.00)	108(90.00)
Foot wear	78 (65.00)	42(35.00)

Note: Figures in brackets represent % age.

Table—5.27: Number of possession of clothing and foot wearing among street children

Range of holding (in Nos.)	*Pant (N = 118)*	*Shirt/T-shirt (N = 108)*	*Winter clothing (N = 12)*	*Foot wear (N = 78)*
1-2	68(57.63)	48(44.44)	12(100.00)	78(100.00)
3-4	24(20.34)	40(37.04)	–	–
5-6	12(10.17)	18(16.67)	–	–
7+	4 (3.39)	2 (1.85)	–	–

Table—5.28: Number of street children exchanging dresses with their brothers/sisters

Category	*Total sample*	*Have brothers/sisters with whom exchange of dress is possible*	*Exchange*	*Do not exchange*
Boys	90	68 (100.00)	38 (55.88)	30 (44.12)
Girls	30	16 (100.00)	8 (50.00)	8 (50.00)
Total	**120**	**84 (100.00)**	**46 (54.76)**	**38 (45.24)**

Note: Figures in brackets represent % age.

Table—5.29: Quality of cleanliness of dress the among street children

Category of cleanliness	*Total cases*	*% age*
Very very unclean	51	42.50
Very unclean	46	38.33
Unclean	14	11.67
Clean	9	7.50
Total	**120**	**100.00**

Table—5.30: Future perspectives of the street children

Sl. No.	*Purpose*	*Total cases*	*% age*
1.	Stick to the present job	48	40.00
2.	To be a rickshaw/trolley puller	27	22.5
3.	Wage-earner/coolie	22	18.33
4.	Vending	7	5.83
5.	Petty business	5	4.17
6.	Garage/mechanical assistant/ motor vehicle helper	10	8.33
7.	Beggary	1	0.83
	Total	**120**	**100.00**

Table—5.31: Whom do the Street Children Blame for their Present Plight (N = 120)

Sl. No.	*Variables*	*Total cases*	*% age*
1.	Father	75	62.5
2.	Mother	3	2.50
3.	Poverty	25	20.83
4.	Broken family	3	2.50
5.	Peers	3	2.50
6.	Bad luck	6	5.00
7.	Tradition	4	3.33
8.	Death of partners	3	2.50
	No answer	9	7.50

Table—5.32: Interest among street children towards receiving free education with free lodging and boarding facility

Variables	*Total cases*	*% age*
Interested	44	36.67
Non interested	76	63.33
Total	**120**	**100.00**

Table—5.33: Aspirations among interested street children after being educated (N = 44)

Aspirations (1)	*Total cases* (2)	*% age* (3)	*Remarks* (4)
Teacher	4	9.09	
Petty business	15	34.09	Book selling-1 Cycle shop-1 Shoe shop-4 Tailoring-7 Tea shop-2
Salaried job	3	6.82	Constable-1 inspector-2
Mechanic/garage work/ driving of motor vehicles	12	27.27	Driver-5 Mechanic-7

(Contd...)

(1)	(2)	(3)	(4)
Salesman in grocery shop	1	2.27	–
To improve quality of life	1	2.27	–
Wage-earning	2	4.55	Trolley-1 domestic servant
To avail better job opportunity	1	2.27	–
No answer	5	11.36	

Table—5.34: Harassment by public, police, municipal official to the street children during last year (N = 120)

Variables	*Harassed*	*Not harassed*
Public	16 (13.33)	104 (86.67)
Municipal Officials	4 (3.33)	116 (96.67)
Railway/public police	9 (7.5)	111 (92.50)

Note: Figures in brackets represent % age.

Table—5.35: Feeling about present life among street children (N = 120)

Feeling	*Total cases*	*% age*
Good	61	50.83
Bad	20	16.62
Unsecured	2	1.67
Disappointed	7	5.83
Helpless	6	5.00
Gloomy about figure	10	8.33
No answer	14	11.67

6

Legislation, Welfare Programmes and the Street Children

Pre and Post Independence Legislation

The problems of street children can be traced back to the time when the Britishers came to India established some trading centres at different places of the country. But the problem of these children was felt by them much later towards the end of their administration in India. However, some of the relevant legislations which had been passed and implemented from time to time during their administration were mainly concerned to the eradication of child labour. These legislative measures include the *Indian Factories Act of 1881, the Minor Act of 1901, Factories Act of 1911, Indian ports Act of 1931, the Tea Districts Emigrant Labour Act of 1932, the children (pledging of labour) Act of 1933, Employment of children Act of 1938 etc.* All these Acts more or less specify the age of work and working hours per day but these do not concern much to the street children who work on streets either being pressurised by their parents or because of some other unavoidable reasons.

After the colonial administration in India, concerted efforts were made to eradicate the age-old problems attached to the poor and destitute children working in various fields. When the constitution was being formulated, the gravity of this problem was felt and it was placed in the "Directive Principles of the State Policy", which specifies that the state shall in particular direct its policy towards securing a healthy life by the way that the children are given opportunities and facilities to develop in healthy manner and in conditions of freedom and dignity and that childhood and youth are protected against exploitation and against moral and material abandonment (Art 39, constitution of India). Subsequently in order to give a fruitful shape to this policy, both the central and state governments enacted and introduced various Articles and policies. Some of the major policies and Acts which emerged after deep thoughts among the administrators and legislators are: *Right of Children—1959, Motor Vehicle Transport Workers Act 1961, National Policy for Children 1974 National Health Policy 1982, Juvenile Justice Act 1986, Child labour (prohibition and regulation) Act, 1986, National Policy of Education 1986, Infant Milk Substituting Feeding Bottles and Infant Food Act 1992, National Policy on Nutrition 1993* etc. (cf. Mandal, 1990; 64-118, Phillips, 1994; 155-64, G.O.O., 1995; 7 and G.O.O., 1995: 1).

Some of the policies and Acts which had been introduced by the Britishers were either retained or modified in different Acts in post independence period but unfortunately no specific and pinpointed Act had yet been made to protect the rights of the street children as a whole and at the same time to tackle the problems attached to their parents and their personal situations.

United Nations Convention on Rights of the Child and National Plan of Action

In the United Nation's General Assembly Meeting held in 1989, the rights of the child were discussed and the results were unanimously accepted for protection of the child against negligence, abuse and exploitation. The convention specified that the child should be enabled by law and other means to develop physically, mentally, morally, spiritually in a healthy and normal manner and in conditions of freedom and dignity. It also further proclaimed that the child has the right to adequate nutrition, housing, recreation and medical services (cf. G.O.I, 1995; 1-2; G.O.I, 1993-8). But it raises a question mark in the mind of a lay man as to how a street child is a 'child' and what the rights to adequate food, nutrition, housing, clothing, recreation and medical services mean to it unless the legislation on these aspects are properly implemented? A street child roams or works on street for earning his/her own bread. Can he/she have the right to take adequate nutrition from a public on the road or from his/her parents who spend time in utter poverty? A child who does not own a house and spends nights in railway platforms or under open sky, how can he/she demand for a roof? Who will him/her? A child who looks unkempt, hated by the public and not even allowed to enter into the public parks and to use a common swing, how can he/she have the right for recreation? A child who is not aware about his/her personal hygienic condition and does not have any guardian to take care of him/her, how can he/she raise his/her demand for medical service? Hence, this convention does not provide anything specific for the eradication of the problems of the street children as a whole. But in pursuance of the above objectives of the convention on the rights of the child, Government of India has formulated an action plan on some broad areas as mentioned below:

(i) Reduction of Infant Mortality Rate (IMR) to less than 60 thousand live births and reduction of Child Mortality Rate (CMR) to less than 10 by 2000 A.D.;

(ii) Reduction of Maternal Mortality Rate (MMR) by half in between 1990 to 2000 A.D.;

(iii) Reduction in service as well as moderate malnutrition among children under 5 years of age by half of 1990 levels;

(iv) *(a)* Arrangement of potable water source within a distance of one km., horizon and 50 meters elevation difference;

(b) One spot source standpoint for 100/150 persons;

(v) Universal enrolment, retention, minimum level of learning, reduction of disparities and universalisation of access to schooling; and

(vi) Improvement in protection of children in especially difficult circumstances. (cf. G.O.O., 1993: 7-8).

Thus, from the above broad objectives of the Union government, the last two are more or less directly related to the welfare of the street children. In accordance with these two specific objectives, Ministry of Welfare, Government of India, has already started a provision of a mega welfare scheme for these children. The scheme covers financial assistance to various government and Non-Government Organisations (NGOs) for providing integrated community-based and non-institutional basic services for the care, protection and development of the street children facing destitution, neglect, abuse and exploitation. The specific components of this scheme are as follows:

(i) Identification of street children and their families found at the risk of disorganisation, abuse or exploitation,

(ii) Mobilisation of preventive health services, treatment facilities and providing access to the marginalised children 'of' and 'on' the street,

(iii) Providing nutritions support to maintain the requisite level of physical and mental efficiency of the street children,

(iv) Offering facilities for literacy, numeracy and life education and initiating efforts for mainstreaming in the formal education,

(v) Linking facilities for the training of street children in gainful vocations, trades and skills so as to enhance their earning capacity,

(vi) Utilising and promoting facilities for shelter and hygienic living,

(vii) Offering counselling, guidance and referral services for upgrading the quality of life among the street children,

(viii) Providing organised recreation for a healthy, harmonious and wholesome growth of the street children,

(ix) Making all possible efforts for the reintegration of street children with their families or their placement in a family setting,

(x) Promotion of entrepreneurship among street children for income-generation wherever necessary by mobilising facilities of institutional credit, and

(xi) Protecting street children against all forms of abuse and exploitation (G.O.I, 1990: 1-2).

State Plan of Action for Children by 2000 A.D.

In agreement with the above objectives of the Union government, the Government of Orissa has formulated a plan of action for the development of the children of various categories with an objective to achieve the goals by 2000 A.D. It covers some broad goals on improvement of child and maternal health, provision of nutritional facility, universalisation of primary education, provision of drinking water, environmental sanitation, eradication of child labour and legal provisions of rights of the child, specific programmes for girl children with emphasis on the adolescent girls, special package for urban children and coverage of children especially in difficult circumstances in specific sectorial welfare measures. Some of the major and specific objectives that are included in the State Plan of Action for children are as follows:

(i) Reduction of Infant Mortality Rate (IMR) to less than 60 per thousand live births by 2000 A.D.,

(ii) Reduction of Maternal Mortality Rate (MMR) by 50 per cent of 1995 by 2000 A.D.,

(iii) Reduction of severe and moderate malnutrition among children under 5 years of age,

(iv) Achievement of universal primary education for all children in the age group of 6-14 years of age,

(v) Universal access to save drinking water by the way of provision of one hand pump for a population of 150 in all villages and hamlets by 2000 A.D.,

(vi) Eliminating child labour under 14 years of age in all hazardous industries by 2000 A.D.,

(vii) Improvement in the status of the girl children,

(viii) Coverage of immunization of preventable diseases and to sustain 100 per cent coverage by 2000 A.D.,

(ix) Ensuring 100 per cent identification of disadvantaged urban children and their registration and sustaining the achievement by 2000 A.D.,

(x) Providing protection care and development to the children especially in difficult circumstances, (G.O.O, 1985: 2-3).

With the above objectives, the Orissa State Plan of Action for Children by 2000 A.D., was launched by the honourable Chief Minister of the state Shri J.B. Patnaik on September 4, 1995 at Soochana Bhawan. In his speech, the Chief Minister said that the overall implementation of this plan of Action for the welfare of children involves the co-ordinated efforts of teachers, health workers, aganwadi workers and other grass-root level functionaries, voluntary organisations, training and research institutions, mahila mandals, women activists, mass media etc. The plan of Action also takes an integrated and holistic view of all measures necessary to achieve the goals and calls for co-ordinated endeavor of government and Non-government agencies. In furtherance of this plan, Orissa Government has envisaged a state level Task Force with the Chief Secretary as its chair-person and representatives of various Departments of Government and Voluntary Organisations as members to monitor, review and oversee the implementation of the 'Plan of Action' as well as the resource management (cf. G.O.O, 1995: 3).

If some of the above objectives, which seem to have related to the welfare of the street children in general are discussed, the broad objectives of 'eradication of child labour' and 'rights of child' pin point that elimination of child labour under 14 years of age in all hazardous industries and withdrawal of children under 12 years of age from all category of industries are the prime sectorial goals and these objectives have been specified to the fulfilled by the end of 2000 A.D. And for the rehabilitation of child labourers, people are being sensitised about the rights of the child and sustained efforts are being made to re-unite of the disadvantaged children to their families. As regards to the rights of the child, actions are being sustained to provide the disadvantaged children their basic rights to their family.

For the welfare of urban children residing in Municipal and NAC areas, all sectoral plans (on nutrition, education etc.) are being extended to them. In addition to this, identification of all disadvantaged urban children and their registration through a sustained effort is being made and provision of basic facilities of shelter, drinking water, sanitation and health care etc. are being made for them.

For the overall welfare of the street children, the other strategic plans include identification of *at risk* poor urban families, assessment of their socio-economic status, preparation of city/town action plan for the children residing in urban areas, maintenance of birth and death registration at the base level and effective implementation of all urban poverty alleviation scheme, coverage of immunization for all antigens, supply of supplementary nutrition, iron folic tablets and vitamin 'A' solution, ensuring of growth monitoring in *'slums areas'* and provide counselling and support service to the identified *'children at risk'*, ensuring of attendance of all children in the age group of 6-11 in primary schools etc. (cf. G.O.O. 1995: 15-84).

Welfare Agencies and On-going Action Plans in Bhubaneswar City

In order to implement various plans and programmes for the welfare and development of the children in general and the street children in particular in different cities and towns of Orissa, a state level agency called, Orissa State Council for Child Welfare (OSCCW) was constituted and established on 5th November, 1989. It is affiliated to the Indian Council for Child Welfare (ICCW), New Delhi and runs under Women and Child Development Department of the Government of Orissa. The main objectives of the council as mentioned in the Orissa State Council for Child Welfare (Amendment) Rules, 1996 are as follows:

(a) To undertake welfare work for children, adolescents and expectant and nursing mothers without any discrimination;

(*b*) To arrange proper education of children for their moral, spiritual, cultural and social development;

(*c*) To encourage aesthetic appreciation, artistic taste, constructive imagination and creativity amongst the children;

(*d*) To initiate, undertake and promote either directly or indirectly various schemes and projects for furtherance of child welfare;

(*e*) To organise and maintain institutions for rehabilitation of orphans, abandoned and destitute children and for the training of child welfare workers, volunteers and organisers;

(*f*) To publish and propagate the literature relating to child welfare;

(*g*) To co-operate and/or collaborate with national and international organisations having similar objectives and to depute or receive representatives to and from such organisations;

(*h*) To co-operate with other agencies, both governmental and non-governmental ogranisations and administration of schemes and funds for furtherance of child welfare; and

(*i*) To fulfil the objectives and implement the policies and programmes of the Indian Council of Child Welfare.

As per the annual report 1996-97 of the Orissa State Council for Child Welfare, at present the council implements 7 different welfare schemes for the benefit of the children of the state. These schemes include functioning of 6 Balashrams at 6 districts (Appendix: 6) in order to provide proper care and rehabilitation of orphan and destitute children of various parts of Orissa; functioning of one 'Vocational Training Centre' at Barang for providing training and rehabilitation of the handicapped persons; running of 5 'Anganwadi Training Centres' for providing effective technical training inputs for a number of anganwadi workers; functioning of 44 'Creches' all over the state through 21 local voluntary organisations; functioning of 6 centres for the rehabilitation of *street children;* functioning of 4 centres or shelters in order to provide proper care for *unprotected children* and their subsequent rehabilitation; and functioning of one children's health centre at Puri for providing medical services to the children of fishermen community. The council also recommends *destitute* and *orphan children* of various voluntary organisations for adoption within and outside the country (Appendix: 6).

At present the council runs 6 centres at Bhubaneswar city (FCI malgodown, Railway Station, Santinagar, Laxmisagar Sikharchandi and Ainginia) for the rehabilitation of the street children under a sponsored project of the Ministry of Human Resource Development (HRD) Department, Government of India. The scheme aims at providing education to the street children and their rehabilitation. Under this scheme, the street children get some nutritional incentives like bread, banana etc., at the end of all classes everyday.

The said council also operates a similar scheme for the rehabilitation of the street children and the children in difficult circumstances, at Sambalpur, Cuttack and Bhubaneswar under financial assistance from Government of Orissa. The main objective of this project is to take care of the *unprotected children* and their subsequent rehabilitation. During the year of (1996-97), a total number of 150 unprotected children have been assisted under the scheme. The total achievement of the council under this scheme is presented in Appendix No. 7.

Apart from Orissa State Council for Child Welfare, among a number of Bhubaneswar based nodal autonomous Non-Government Organisations (NGOs), very few work as forefront action planners for the development and welfare of the street children in Bhubaneswar city. Among those, the important ones are and Ruchika Social Service Wing (RSSW), Centre for Youth and Social Development (CYSD), Council of Professional Social Workers (CPSW) etc. Each of these organisations has its own welfare schemes.

Ruchika Social Service wing has a number of sectoral schemes, like elimination of child labour, provision of food, bath at nominal rates, provision of recreation, provision of functional education etc. for the development and welfare of street as well as abandoned, orphan and runaway children. Under the elimination of child labour scheme, it operates 16 railway platform schools at places, like Bhubaneswer, Barang, Balasore, Chandanpur, Cuttack, Puri, Jajpur, Khurdha etc. where the street children are imparted 'Non-formal Education' (NFE) for 3 hours a day. Learning is imparted through various attractive methods, like performing drama, dance, puppet shows and singing songs.

Drop-in-Shelter (DIS) at Bhubaneswar seems to be a very helpful scheme for the abandoned, orphan and runaway children in the age group of 8-18 years. Under this scheme, a child is free to avail 3 meals a day at subsidised rates, bathing facility at nominal cost, sleeping facility, indoor and outdoor games, non-formal education, medical aid rehabilitation through vocational training etc.

A vocational training centre is also being operated by the above organisation for the working street and slum children who are above 14 years of age. Some important vocational trades which are being introduced for the welfare of these children include tailoring, laundry work, shoe-making and hotel utilities. The trainees are provided with a monthly stipend of Rs. 200/- per head and it is saved in their personal savings account in order to enable them to establish their own trade units after the training is over.

For the entertainment purpose the organisation provides a toy library for the street children and also extends medical services for treatment of various causal diseases, like skin ailments, ear and eye infection etc.

Centre for Youth and Social Development (CYSD), as a national level Bhubaneswar based voluntary organisation also works for the slum children. It extends various welfare programmes on formal and non-formal education, preventive health care, cultural and recreational activities at different slums namely Dumuduma, Bharatpur, Sikharchandi, Saliashai, Patharabandha, Dhirikuti and Trinath Basti of Bhubaneswar city. Apart from these programmes, it also provides potable water through tap and tube well systems at Dumuduma and Sikharachandi (Verbal discussion with the chief, PLAN Project, CYSD, on 15 the April, 1998).

Campaign Against Child Labour (CACL) is a national network. It has a chapter in Orissa for complete eradication of child labour in the state Council for Professional Social Workers (CPSW), a Bhubaneswar based voluntary organisation is convening and co-ordinating the programme in Orissa through about 200 active individual members and 400 member organisation of the state.

This programme has set up a strategy for eradication of child labour in the state through networking, campaign, advocacy, lobbying and rehabilitation activities of the volunteers. It has also set a goal to make Bhubaneswar city child-labour free within few years. It has recently completed a massive door to door survey in slums and also business establishments where the child labourers are found to work. (cf. CPSW News, 1998: 16 and Call Orissa News, 1998: 2-11).

Thus, from the above discussions it becomes clear that a number of attempts have been made for the welfare of the slum children in general and street children in particular during post independence period but not much has yet been achieved satisfactorily. Even to-day, after about 55 years of independence of our country the problems of these children have remained unchanged. The behaviour of the employers of these children at hotels, garages, shops etc. seem to be very inhuman in most of the cases and the legislation and the existing laws have no impact at all. Most of these children do not get proper nutrition and hence are malnutriated and medical care is almost nil for them. As a result of this, the investigators have not come across a single street child who looked healthy and well dressed while working on them during the survey period. So we have to be very cautious and serious about implementing the existing plans and programmes with a view to achieving the real goal successfully. Some of the constructive suggestive measures are given in the next chapter for the welfare of these children.

7

A Recipe for Development of Street Children

The root cause of any social problem lies on sustained persistence of an imbalance between population and available resources for utilisation. In a populous country like India, human population is growing very fast because of illiteracy, low level of awareness among the rural people and flexible implementation of family planning legislations. It exerts much pressure on the available resources, and when the resources become scarce, people face various problems and migrate to no resourceful areas in order to extract their livelihood. Developing urban centres are such resourceful areas that pull a number of rural wage-earning people. But when the urban centres receive more of such people than required, the available resources are over exploited and in such situations most of the children of these people come on to the streets to work and earn their own livelihood. As a result, in order to have complete eradication of appearance of these children on streets of urban centres, on priority basis, our national family planning measures should be implemented with utmost sincerity instead of being suggestive to have only one or two children per couple. This would, in the other way, minimise over migration of poor rural people to different developing urban centres and hence proper balance between population and resources for utilisation could be maintained. The other related suggestive measures for immediate adoption and implementation for eradication of street children would be as follows:

(*a*) That the municipal corporate bodies must develop their own strategic measures to restrict over immigration of rural wage-earners whose children most often come on to the streets for work. These corporate bodies must be very cautious to register each immigrant and not to accommodate more immigrants than required. It should endeavour to rehabilitate them properly.

(*b*) Those who are accommodated within the municipal area and there provided with Urban Basic Service (UBS) facilities, must be imparted awareness to strictly follow the family planning measures of the government. In no case a family residing within the municipality be permitted to procreate more children than approved. Those who fail to follow it should be withdrawn from availing accommodation and land holding facility within the municipal boundary. If, for the time being, these suggestive recommendations are not possible for implementation, then the following measures be adopted for the development and welfare of the street children.

(*c*) That a scientific survey be made on priority basis to identify Street-Child-households. In each slum, these children must be covered under universalisation of formal education and it should be looked that they are not asked or imposed by their parents to work as earners either on streets or on any other places. If it happens so, then their parents must be restricted from availing ration-card facility or be withdrawn from poverty alleviation programmes if they are covered under any such programmes.

(*d*) Each and every child of the slum must be provided with free education apart from the free boarding facility, at least upto matriculation and there should be job guarantee for the matriculates. For the non-matriculates, need-based vocational training be provided according to their own choices and demand of the market. Provision should also be made for rehabilitation of successful trainees so that more and more street children as well as their parents would be interested and come forward to avail of the opportunities. By this way, two-fold objectives of the nation, viz. improvement of literacy and reduction of unemployment among the Indian population would be considerably reduced.

(e) The poorest of the poor at *'At-Risk'* slum dwellers and those who live on footpaths, under open sky, railway platforms, market complex premises, office premises etc. should be identified on priority and be covered under special poverty alleviation programmes in order to improve their economic condition. These children should be given more attention and be covered under the above job-guaranteed educational and vocational training programmes.

(f) Medical service should be provided at the door step of each and every slum dweller periodically, i.e. at least once in a week through public mobile-health-check up-camps/vans. Emphasis must be given to check up each child and nursing mothers without fail.

(g) Since the nature and working pattern of the street children varies from one to another, government must work out some specific legislations for the welfare of each category of these children. For example, the working nature and pattern of a domestic servants is not same as with a hotel boy or a garage worker. Hence, there must be specific legislations indicating their nature of work, hour of work, etc. Accordingly minimum wage rates be also fixed up and specified in order to protect them from exploitation.

(h) The rag-pickers work hard throughout the day but they are exploited at various levels; one level being at the local godown keepers where they sell their collections. Since there is no uniformity in the rate charts for different rag-items, the innocent rag-pickers fall prey to various godown keepers. So, government must take proper initiatives to fix-up uniform rates for different scraps and the godown keepers must be instructed to display the rate charts for public and work accordingly.

(i) Relating to the above suggestion, there should be a special consumer court to which the children can have easy access and approach to file complains.

(j) As an alternative to the above suggestion (i) it would be better if municipal corporate bodies fix up some collection localities/centres and collect rags from rag-pickers at/from such localities/centres through mobile collection vans. If it is done so, in one hand these corporate bodies would raise their own revenue and on the other hand the rag-pickers would get proper value of their collections and hence also get freed from being exploited by the local godown keepers.

(k) As the street children are deprived of availing public parks, playgrounds etc. for relaxation, slum-based recreational playgrounds be developed and game items be provided by the municipal corporate bodies.

(l) Government should take immediate steps to identify the orphans who work on streets, railway stations etc. on priority basis and must try to accommodate them in orphange homes financed by union or state government or NGOs funded by foreign agencies.

(m) Like the orphans, girl-street children should also be identified on priority basis and specific need-based self employment programmes be formulated for them. Specifically, they should be imparted training on some vocational trades, like sewing, applique work, terra cotta work and other handicrafts out of which they can independently earn their livelihood. However, there must be a co-operative institution at the government level to procure the product from these children at the reasonable cost fixed by the government. This would, in other way help them to get suitable life partners for marriage.

(n) It is universally accepted that if we educate a man, we educate a person but if we educate a woman, we educate a family. So, apart from providing vocational training, girl children should also be provided with formal or non-formal education depending upon their age and interest.

(m) Finally, a special committee be formed at the government level to facilitate proper implementation of the welfare schemes and to protect the street children from exploitation.

8

Summary and Conclusion

Growth of Slums and Street Children

Now-a-days rapid emergence of street children in urbanising centres has become a great concern all over the world, particularly in the third world countries. More specifically in a country, like India, the number of these children is increasing at an alarming rate. Some of the Indian metro cities, like Delhi, Mumbai, Kolkata, Chennai etc. have experienced tremendous growth of these children. But in Orissa, when Bhubaneswar became the state capital in 1948, and thereafter construction work of various official buildings, residential complexes, roads, parks, schools, colleges, cinema halls, hotels, offices etc. were started in full swing, thousands of rural wage-earning people from within the state of Orissa and adjoining states, like Andhra Pradesh, West Bengal, Bihar etc. immigrated into the city so as to avail gainful earning opportunities. Over the years, these people have so far created more than 100 slums in and around the city and also have developed a number of pavement dwellings. Primarily, these people work in various informal sectors, like road and building construction, rickshaw and trolley pulling and operation of other transport vehicles, vending, wage-earning, hawking etc. But the faster of over-population and availability of limited resources within a confined and mechanised ecological niche do not permit them to earn sufficiently for maintaining themselves a sense of 'struggle for self survival' has developed among them and in such a situation, the parents ask their children to work and earn for themselves as well as for others in the family. These children jump over to any work, like rag-picking, shoe-shining, performing domestic service as servants, working in garages and hotels, vending edible items, cleaning railway platforms and train compartments etc. from, which they think, that they can earn something to sustain their lives and also to support others in their families.

In order to have a complete and thorough idea about the life-style of these children, in the present study, a total number of 120 street children of Bhubaneswar city have been studied. Their family background, that is, under which circumstances they have come up to work on streets, their present socio-economic condition and the ways of leading a life and how do they struggle for their survival etc. have been discussed vividly in 3 major chapters, viz. chapter III, IV and V of this book. The main findings of the study are mentioned below under different broad headings.

Category of Street Children

(a) As per the criteria of the United Nations, street children of the person study are categorised into 3 broad groups, viz (i) children on the street, (ii) children of the street, and (iii) Abandoned, destitute or neglected children.

The first category of street children mostly stay with their parents but work throughout the day on streets and go back to their respective homes at the end of each working day. The second category of children are those who have either left their homes out of anguish, torture or suffering and stay at places, like railway platforms, bus stations, abandoned or dilapidated or incomplete constructions, such as building units, market complexes or even under open sky. The third category of children more or less considered as an extension of the second category. But the condition of these children is very serious and hence pitiable as they do not have any chance or scope to meet their parents to get love and affection and also security when they fall prey to others or suffer from any illness.

(b) That of the total 120 sample children, as many as 106 accounting for 89.17 per cent constitute the first category, i.e. 'children on the street'. The second category of children who are termed as 'children of the street' constitute 12 or 10 per cent of the total sample and the rest 2 or 1.67 per cent of children are found to be destitute and hence they form the third category.

Family Background

Family background plays an important role in formation and development of the nature, personality and earning ability of a person. Hence, it was thought important to discuss some of the crucial background information about the family of the street children. The points which have been dealt with in this section includes places from which their parents have migrated, duration of staying in Bhubaneswar city, family size, occupation and education of parents, occupation of brothers and sisters etc.

(a) That in case of 65.83 per cent of street children, their parents have migrated from different districts of the state of Orissa namely Ganjam (30.83%), Jagatsingpur (6.38%), Balasore (5.83%), Cuttack (5.83%), Nayagarh (5.83%), Khurdha (5.00%), Nawarangpur (3.33%), Gajapati (2.50%), Bhadrak (1.67%), and Kendrapada (1.67%). Only 0.83 per cent of them are found to belong to Bhubaneswar city itself. Among the rest, 21.67 per cent have migrated from the state of West Bengal followed by Andhra Pradesh (8.33%) and Bihar (0.83%).

(b) With regard to the period of staying in Bhubaneswar city, highest percentage (24.17%) of them have stayed in the city for about 20 years or more and the rest have recently immigrated into the city within last 20 years.

(c) The family size of the street children is found to be very large. On an average it comes to be 6.34 persons per family.

(*d*) So far as the education of the parents of the street children is concerned, 86.67 per cent of fathers are illiterate as against 96.67 per cent of mothers.

(*e*) Little more than 34 per cent (34.17) of households have been considered as literate households in which at least one literate person is available in each of these households. Among the rest 65.83 per cent of households all the members are found to be illiterate and hence these are treated as illiterate households.

(*f*) Among the total literate households, 70.73 per cent have 1-2 literate members followed by 17.09 and 12.20 per cent of households having 3-4 and 5-6 literate persons per household respectively.

(*g*) Most (29.36%) of the household heads (Fathers) work as wage-earners. Among the rest, 23.85 per cent earn their livelihood out of rickshaw and trolley pulling and 15.60 per cent from rag-picking or keeping of rag godown.

(*h*) Majority (42.99%) of mothers of the street children earn their daily bread out of wage-earning, followed by rag-picking (15.89%), domestic service (18.69%) etc. About 18.7 per cent of them do not work outside their home as wage-earners rather they manage their homes with the income earned by their husbands and children.

(*i*) Among a total number of 292 brothers, about 44 (43.84) per cent work as rag-pickers. Little more than 7.5 per cent are engaged in potato collection from godown sites, followed by 5.48 per cent of them who work as garage boys and helpers at cycle repairing shops. Rest others are shoe-shiners (5.14%) and rickshaw-pullers (4.45%).

(*j*) Out of the total 205 sisters, highest percentage (41.46%) work as rag-pickers, followed by 18.54 per cent domestic servants, 7.32 per cent wage earners, 6 per cent in potato sorting work at daily and weekly markets etc.

Demographic and Socio-economic Profile of the Street Children

(*a*) That irrespective of sex, most (35.00%) of the street children belong to the age group of 13-14 years. But when maximum percentage (36.67%) of girl street children fall in the age group of 9-10 years, it is the age group of 13-14 years in which most (38.80%) of the boy street children are concentrated.

(*b*) That 35 per cent of the street children are born within the Bhubaneswar city itself as against 61.67 per cent who are born outside the city. The rest children do not know about their birth places.

(*c*) As regards the religious affiliation, 70.83 per cent of the street children are found to be Hindu as against 22.5 per cent Muslim and 6.67 per cent do not belong to any modern philosophical religion. They are tribal and as such animistic.

(*d*) Relating to the linguistic/communal affiliation, 31.67 per cent of children comprise Oriya Hindu backward castes, 25 per cent Tamil, 22.5 per cent Muslims, 10.83 per cent Oriya Scheduled Castes, 6.67 per cent Scheduled Tribes, and the rest 0.83 per cent Bengali.

(*e*) As regards to castes, most (65.83%) of the street do not know about their caste background. But those who could tell their caste names comprise 9.17 per cent, *Matia* (Earth cutter), 8.33 per cent, *Mochi* (Cobbler), 6.67 per cent, *Sabar* (a Scheduled Tribe community), 5 per cent *Gauda* (Cattle herder), 1.67 per cent, *Barika* (Barber), 1.67 per cent *Chasa/Khandayat* (Agriculturist/Warrior), 0.83 per cent, *Kumbhara* (Potter), and 0.83 per cent *Tanti* (Weaver).

(*f*) With regard to the living status of the parents of the street children, it can be said that in case of 8.33 per cent of cases the fathers are not alive as against 5.83 per cent who have lost their mothers. One child (0.83%) is found to be an orphan. The rest 85 per cent, however, have both the parents.

(g) That 88.33 per cent of street children stay with their parents but 5.83 per cent regularly stay at the railway platforms. Others stay at abandoned or dilapidated houses (1.67%), market complex premises (1.67%), and garage/hotel premises (1.67%). The rest one child (0.83%) manages to stay with its relative's house.

(h) Among those street children who have left their homes, 43 per cent have been staying outside their homes since last three years or more followed by 35.71 per cent staying outside their homes for about 1-2 years and 21.43 per cent of them are found to have left their homes very recently, i.e. within one year and are staying at places of their own choices.

(i) So far as the factors responsible for staying outside own homes are concerned, 64.29 per cent say that it is because of their anguish, torture, suffering and regular conflict with their parents; mostly with fathers, 21.43 per cent opine that they have left home and are staying at railway platforms as this place is favourable for earning; others pointed out that it was mainly because of the death of their parents (14.29%), lack of sufficient space at home for accommodation of all family members (14.29%), and late night working pattern at working sites (14.29%).

(j) Regarding educational status, about 78 per cent of street children are illiterate and the rest 22 per cent are found to be literate.

(k) That the highest level of education achieved by most of the street children is found to be primary standard.

(l) That a total number of 5 (4.17%) of them are still continuing formal education apart from working on streets.

(m) That a total number of 26 street children accounting for 21.67 per cent are now continuing with Non-formal-Education (NFE) at different NFE centres run by Orissa State Council for Child Welfare and some other organisations. But they are observed to be very irregular in attending classes daily. Most of them remain busy in their work but reach at school just at the time of distribution of foodstuffs.

(n) That the street children of Bhubaneswar city are mainly engaged in as many as 10 different informal sectors, viz rag-picking (55.83%), potato collection from godown sites (12.00%), domestic service (8.33%), shoe shining (8.23%), garage work and helping at cycle repairing shops (5.83%), vending of edible items (3.33%), collection of semi-burnt coal and green coconut fibers (1.67%), hotel work (1.67%), potato sorting (1.67%), and cleaning of railway platforms and train compartments (1.67%).

(o) That highest percentage (57.78) of boys and also girls (50.00%) have adopted rag-picking as their source of livelihood.

(p) That most (62.5%) of the Scheduled Tribe (ST) Street children work as domestic servants, Scheduled Castes (SC) as shoe-shiners (76.92%), Oriya Hindu backward caste as rag-pickers (36.84%) and potato collectors (36.84%), Urdu speaking (Muslims) children as rag-pickers (22.5%). Hence, rag-picking seems to be the most common work among a majority of the street children.

(q) That about 84 per cent street children are practicing their present jobs for last 1-6 years.

(r) That in most (77.50%) of the cases the street children opine that they have adopted their present jobs as per the advice and suggestion or instruction of their parents.

(s) Conversely 29.17 per cent say that it is because of the fact that more peers are engaged in such jobs which attracted them to adopt their present jobs. Interestingly 20 per cent of them opine that they have taken to their present jobs as these are more profitable than other similar ones.

(t) As regards the duration of work during a day, maximum (34.17%) of these children work for 9-10 hours per day on an average to earn their daily bread and also to support their family members. But the children who work in different hotels toil for longer duration which comes to 14 hours per day. Other workers who work for more than 8 hours a day include those who clean railway platforms and train compartments (12.86 hrs.), vendors (10.5 hrs.), rag-pickers (9.57 hrs.), and shoe-shiner (10.5 hrs).

(u) About 38 street children (31.67%) had some occupations, like potato sorting (10.53%), beggary (7.89%), domestic service as servants (5.26%), helping in motor vehicles (5.26%), wage earning (5.26%), garage work (2.67%), hotel work (2.63%), and helping in butcher's shop (2.63%) prior to do their present jobs.

(v) So far as the age at entry into the first job is concerned, 48.33 per cent of them have started working on streets at the age of 7-8 years followed by 38.33 per cent at the age of 5-6 years. Hence the children who have started their first jobs at the age of 7-8 and 5-6 years together constitute more than 85 per cent of the total sample children.

(w) Apart from doing the present occupation, a total number of 9 or 7.5 per cent of them have some subsidiary occupations, like beggary (66.67%), rag-picking (1.67%), and wage-earning (11.11%).

(x) Maximum (36.67%) of the street children earn Rs. 100-200/- per week, but so far as the occupation-wise daily income is concerned, a vendor earns maximum amount that comes to Rs. 41.25 on an average per day, followed by shoe-shiners (Rs. 38.80), hotel workers (Rs. 28.21), potato collectors (Rs. 27.79), rag-pickers (Rs. 22.79), garage workers (12.43), domestic servants (10.26), railway platform and train compartment cleaners (Rs. 8.00) and potato sorters (Rs. 7.00).

Unfortunately a child who collects semi-burnt coal and green coconut fibres earns only Rs. 3.25 per day.

(*y*) That the average daily per capita income irrespective of occupation comes to Rs. 22.93.

(*z*) That 60 per cent of street children give their whole income daily to their parents as against 31.50 per cent who share their income partly with their parents. About 7.5 per cent of the children do not give any amount of their income to their parents.

(*z. i*) Little less than 27 per cent of the street children have saving habit as against the rest 73 per cent who do not save any money.

(*z. ii*) Among those who save money, 43.44 per cent have saved Rs. 31.00 as against 24.67 per cent, 13.71 per cent and 6.55 per cent who have saved in between Rs. 21-30/-, Rs. 11-20/- and Rs. 1-10 respectively.

(*z. iii*) With regard to the mode of saving, maximum (84.38%) save in earthern savings pot and keep it under the custody of their mothers.

Struggle for Survival

(*a*) That as many as 83 parents accounting for 75 per cent consume alcohol and 19.09 per cent of them are presently suffering from diseases, like fever (7 or 33.33%), abdominal pain (5 or 23.80%), headache (4 or 19.05%), asthma (2 or 9.52%), mental abnormality or madness (2 or 9.52%) etc. and in most of the cases (82.08%) they ask their children to work and earn daily for their livelihood as well as to support their family.

(*b*) Surprisingly in case of 24 or 27.59 per cent of children, their parents mount a mental pressure on them by fixing up of some target amount to earn daily.

(c) For a total number of 24 children, the target amount has been fixed by their parents to be earned daily which comes to Rs. 1/- to 10/- for 37.5 per cent of children, Rs. 11/- to Rs. 20/- for 12.5 per cent of children, Rs. 21/- to Rs. 30/- for 20.83 per cent and Rs. 31/- or more for 29.17 per cent of children.

(d) If they do not work as per the advice of their parents and earn accordingly, most often they are scolded (89.53%), at times they are not given adequate food (30.23%), and even in cases (20.93%) food is completely denied. As times doors are also closed for about 7 per cent of them.

(e) Of the total 106 children who stay with their parents 19 or 17.92 per cent have not come to their respective homes out of fear of being beaten up during the last week when they had not worked so as to meet the demand of their fathers.

(f) Of the 19 children who have not come to their home out of fear, about 74 per cent of them have not come for 1-2 days during the last week followed by 15.79 per cent and 10.53 per cent who have stayed outside their homes for 3 and 4 days respectively.

(g) In such cases 14 or 73.68 per cent stay at the railway platforms, 3 or 15.79 per cent at market complexes, 1 or 5.26 per cent at community halls, meeting pendals of basti/slum etc.

(h) A total number of 103 (93.17%) say that their income is spent towards the general purpose of the family.

(i) That about 13.33 per cent of children had not taken breakfast on the day before the interview was conducted. Surprisingly, 1.67 per cent had no other way than to spend the whole day without a lunch. Further 4.17 per cent could not have dinner before they slept last night. Only 55.83 per cent children had some snacks in between lunch and dinner.

(j) Among those who had breakfast, lunch, tiffin and dinner, about 51 (50.96) per cent say that the quantity of breakfast they consumed was inadequate. Further lunch was not adequate for about 28 per cent of them, followed by 25.22 per cent of children who claimed that they had not taken diner up to their satisfaction. Consumption of tiffin was inadequate for more than 37.31 per cent of them.

(k) That a total number of 58 children, accounting for 48.33 per cent, are addicted to different narcotics, like betel (60.34%), *Khaini* (27.59%), *bidi*/cigar 24.14%) and alcohol/liquor (12.07%).

(l) That a total number of 30 street children, accounting for 25.0 per cent, are presently suffering from various diseases or ailments, like scribes (30.00%), ulcer on feet and body (26.67%), cold and caugh (23.33%), joint pain (20.00%), mild fever (10.00%), polio (3.33%), and tuberculosis (3.33%).

(m) Of these diseased children, for about 73 per cent of them no treatment is being carried out. However, only for 13.33 per cent of children, their parents are consulting with the doctors. A total number of 2 (6.67%) children are under the treatment of the local traditional healers.

(n) That of the total number of street children who have suffered from some diseases, at least one-time checking during the last 2 years, constitute as many as 92 or 76.67 per cent of the total sample. The major diseases from which these children suffered are found to be viral fever (42.39%), scabies (36.00%), cold and caught (31.52%), fever (19.57%), diarrhoea (17.39%), ulcer on feet and body (10.87%), etc.

(o) That a total number of 35 (29.17%) street children are found to be irregular in cleaning their teeth daily as against 47 (39.17%) of them who do not regularly take bath.

(*p*) That in most of the cases (65.83%) these children are found to have short but unclean nails. Those who have short and clean nails constitute only 1.25 per cent of the total sample.

(*q*) That a total number of 108 or 90 per cent of street children do not possess any winter clothing as against 42 or 35.00 per cent who have no foot-wears. Even 2 or 1.67 per cent of them do not have any lower garment of their own to wear and 8 or 6.67 per cent lack shirts to cover up their body. In that cases they use the dress of their brothers or sisters depending upon the situation.

(*r*) That among the boys, 38 or 55.88 per cent and among the girls, 8 or 50 per cent exchange dress materials with their brothers or sisters with whom it is possible.

(*s*) So far as the cleanliness of their daily wearing is concerned, it is very very unclean for 51 or 42.50 per cent, very unclean for 46 or 38.33 per cent and unclean for 11.67 per cent of children. Only 9 or 7.50 per cent of them are, however, found to wear clean dress on the day interview was made with them.

(*t*) Relating to the future perspectives, 40 per cent of children say that they would stick to their present jobs, followed by 22.5 per cent who say that they would become rickshaw/trolley pullers, 18.33 per cent opined that they would work as wage-earner, 8.33 per cent told that they would earn their livelihood out of working in garages or cycle repairing shops, 5.93 per cent are hopeful that they would do some vending business and 4.17 per cent say that they would be able to do some petty business. Very desperately one child (0.83%) says that there is no other way from him than to become a beggar in future.

(*u*) When a question on their present plight was asked, most (62.50%) of them blamed their fathers. 20.83 per cent asserted that it was because of their grim poverty.

The other reasons which were focussed as responsible factors of their present misery were bad luck (5.50%), broken family (2.50%) and influence of peers (2.50%).

Educational Choice and Aspirational Level

(a) That presently 44 or 36.67 per cent of street children are interested to get educated if it is provided with free of cost along with free lodging and board facilities.

(b) Subsequently when a question was asked about their future perspectives after they are educated, 15 or 34.09 per cent of them told that they would raise their capital for doing some business, followed by 12 or 27.27 per cent who opted for becoming technical assistants at motor cycle garages or becoming drivers. About 9.09 per cent or 4 of them were found to be very realistic to adopt teaching profession and 3 or 6.82 per cent hoped that they would like to undertake some salaried jobs.

Attitude of the Public Towards the Street Children

(a) In most of the cases (86.67%) the attitude of the public has been indifferent for these children during the last year. But 13.33 per cent of them say that they have been put into trouble by the public as they become suspects in the eyes of them during loss of their articles from within homes, backyards or around them. In such cases they are scolded, beaten up or even at times handed over to the police. Municipal Officers have harassed a total number of 4 (3.33%) of them by throwing out their articles or ceasing those if they open their small mobile shops, on road sides in crowded areas. Likewise 9 (7.5%) claim that the railway police do not permit them to open their shops at railway stations when Ministers or any other such VIPs come.

(b) However, even though the street children face a number of problems in their day to day life, 60 or

50.83 per cent feel good about their present life. The rest feel bad (20 or 6.67%), gloomy about future (10 or 8.33%), disappointed (7 or 5.83%), helpless (6 or 5.00%) and insecured (2 or 1.67%).

The problems of the street children have been felt both by the government and NGO sectors and at various points of time, different legislative and welfare measures have been taken up by them for the welfare of these children. But even after 57% years of independence of our country, not much has yet been achieved in this obnoxious area. It is surprising to note that during the course of the fieldwork there was not a single street child who was looking healthy. It was very unfortunate for the investigators that they had never come across of any street child with healthy physique, well-dressed and in jolly mood. So instead of simply formulating a number of plans and programmes for the betterment and welfare of these children, much care should be taken up for the proper implementation of these measures, if at all, we are to completely eradicate this problem from the society. These children be provided with all facilities to lead their childhood, which is very essential to promote healthy citizens of our country.

Appendix—1

NABAKRUSHNA CHOUDHURY CENTRE FOR DEVELOPMENT STUDIES, ORISSA

Socio-Economic Condition of Street Children in Bhubaneswar City

(Please put a '✓' mark wherever applicable)

1. Name:
2. Age:
3. Sex: Male./Female
4. Community: ST/SC/OBC/General
5. Caste/Tribe: Sub-caste/Sub-Tribe:
6. Religion:
7. Present Address:
8. Native Place/Permanent Address:
9. Family Background:

Sl. No.	*Name*	*Age*	*Sex*	*Relation with household head*	*Marital status*	*Education*	*Occupation*
(1)	(2)	(3)	(4)	(5)	(6)	(7)	(8)
1.							
2.							

(Contd...)

3.
4.
5.
6.

10. Night Shelter/Residence:
    - *(a)* Staying with parents at home
    - *(b)* Railway platform
    - *(c)* Bust station
    - *(d)* Open market complex
    - *(e)* Pavement
    - *(f)* Under incomplete constructions
    - *(g)* Any other (please specify)
11. Since when you have been staying on street/these places?
12. What are the factors that led you to stay on street/these places?
    - *(a)* Lack of home and as my parents are staying at these places
    - *(b)* Lack of sufficient space at home
    - *(c)* Death of parents/desertion of parents
    - *(d)* Left home out of anguish/suffering/torture
    - *(e)* Self decision to lead independent life
    - *(f)* Influence of peer groups
    - *(g)* Any other please specify

Occupation

13. Your present occupation:
    - *(a)* Rag-picking
    - *(b)* Shoe-cleaning/shining
    - *(c)* Cleaning of motor vehicles

(*d*) Cleaning of railway platform and railway compartments

(*e*) Announcing bus timing and collecting passengers

(*f*) Vendor

(*g*) Begging

(*h*) Any other (please specify)

14. Total no. of years of doing this work:

15. Occupations prior to this work:

16. Age at entry into the first work:

17. Factors responsible for taking to the present work:

(*a*) As per opinion/suggestions of the parents

(*b*) It is more profitable

(*c*) More peers are engaged in this work

(*d*) It is less hazardous

(*e*) Forced by circumstance

(*f*) Any other (please specify)

18. Your working hours: (please describe)

Income and Expenditure: (Daily/weekly/monthly and savings if any)

19. Your income during last 7 days

(*a*) 1st day

(*b*) 2nd day

(*c*) 3rd day

(*d*) 4th day

(*e*) 5th day

(*f*) 6th day

(*g*) 7th day

20. What do you do with your daily income?

    (a) Whole income is given to the parents (Mother/Father)

    (b) Part of the income is given to the parents and the rest is kept with self

    (c) Whole income is kept with self (with any other person)

21. If you keep either the whole of your income or part of it with you, how do you spend it?

    (a) Purpose edible items/narcotics/clothing for self

    (b) Take meal (when regularly)

    (c) Any other (please specify)

22. Do you save any money? Yes/No. If yes, how?

23. How do your parents spend your income?

    (a) Spend for the general purpose of the family

    (b) For majority of times father takes it to consume alcoholic drinks

    (c) At times father takes it to consume alcoholic drinks

Nourishment/Food

24. Consumption pattern

Sl. No.		*Time*	*Place*		*Items consumed*	*Amount spend (if at stall/ hotel*	*Consumed adequately*	*It was inadequate*
			at home	*at stall/ hotel*				
(1)	(2)	(3)	(4)	(5)	(6)	(7)	(8)	(9)
1. Breakfast								
2. Lunch								
3. Tiffin (Evening)								
4. Dinner								

25. Do your parents compel you to earn a fixed amount of money daily? If yes, what is the target amount fixed for to-day or for the last day?

26. If you fail to earn the target amount fixed by your parents, what happens to you?

    (a) Father/Mother does not give food on that day at the end of the work.

    (b) Father/Mother does not give adequate food on that day at the end of the work.

    (c) Father/Mother scolds/beats and threats not to repeat in again.

    (d) Any other (please specify).

27. Have you ever not returned to your home when you have failed to reach the target amount of income fixed by your parents? Yes/No. If yes how many times last month and where do you stay in that case?

Education/Aspiration Levels

28. What is education, what is schooling and what is its utility?

29. Do you feel that you have been admitted to a school? Yes/No.

30. Had you ever admitted in any educational institution? Yes/No. If yes, are you still continuing your education or a drop out?

31. Factors responsible for discontinuing education

    (a) Poor economic condition

    (b) Father/Mother pushed me to do this work

    (c) Lack of books/study materials

    (d) No peer groups

    (e) Fear of teachers

    (f) Any other (Please specify)

32. What your present occupation/work, how do you foresee/plan your future life?

    (a) To be a rickshaw puller

(*b*) Stick to this job

(*c*) Wage-earner

(*d*) Coolie

(*e*) Hotel boy

(*f*) Intend to acquire an useful skill/trade/craft

(*g*) Any other (Please specify)

33. Whom do you blame for your present plight?

34. If government provides free education with free lodging and boarding facility, would you like to leave this occupation/ work and get educated? Yes/No.

35. If yes, what do you do after being educated? (Please specify the job)

Health and Hygiene

36. Do your parents (father/mother) suffer from any disease? (Chronic or any other)? Yes/No. If yes, name the disease.

37. Do you suffer from any disease? Yes/No. If yes, please specify.

38. How long you are suffering from this disease?

39. What are the treatments going on?

    (*a*) No treatment

    (*b*) Consultation with doctor

    (*c*) Consultation with local (community) healer

    (d) Any other (please specify)

40. Name the diseases you have ever suffered during the last 3 years

41. Do you take bath daily? Yes/No. If no, how many times you have not taken bath last week and where do you take your bath?

42. Do you clean your teeth regularly? Yes/No. If no., how many times you have not cleared your teeth last week? How do you clean your teeth and tongue?

43. Status of Nail (observation)
    (a) Short and clean
    (b) Short and unclean
    (c) Long and clean
    (d) Long and unclean
44. No. of dress materials you have
    (a) Pant
    (b) Shirt/T Shirt
    (c) Slipper (foot wear)
    (d) Any other (Please specify)
45. Quality and cleanliness of garments? (observation)
    (a) Very very unclean,
    (b) Very unclean,
    (c) Unclean,
    (d) Clean.
46. From which source you have got these dress materials?
    (a) Purchased from the market
    (b) Collected as gift from the public
    (c) Any other (please specify)
47. Do you exchange your dresses between/among
    (a) Your brothers
    (b) Your sisters
    (c) Your brothers and sisters
    (d) Your friends

Harassment by Police, Municipal Officials and Public

48. Any restriction imposed on you by police/municipal officials or any public not to do your business here? Yes/No.

49. Have you ever been arrested by the police and held at police station? Yes/No. If yes, why?

50. Have they harassed you like torture, eviction, imprisonment etc.? Yes/No., If yes, how?

51. Does any local goon collect *bati* from you? Yes/No., If yes, frequency and amount?

Basic Requirements

Please rank the following eight basic requirements on priority basis.

(1) Education

(2) Clothes

(3) Food

(4) Shelter

(5) Medical treatment

(6) Security

(7) Employment

(8) Causal earning

52. What do you feel about your present life?

(a) Good,

(b) Bad,

(c) Insecured,

(d) Disappointed,

(e) Helpless,

(f) Gloomy about future.

53. Major assets available at your home

(a) Income generating	Non-income generating
(i)	*(i)*
(ii)	*(ii)*
(iii)	*(iii)*
(iv)	*(iv)*

Appendix—2

List of slums in Bhubaneswar Municipal Corporation, 1997.

Sl. No.	*Name of the slum*	*Total household*	*Population*	*Family size*
(1)	(2)	(3)	(4)	(5)
1.	Huda Bhoi Sai	92	339	3.68
2.	Nalamunha Sai	21	65	3.10
3.	Jayadev Nagar	66	278	4.21
4.	Mati Bhoi Sai	30	81	2.7
5.	Badagada Bhoi Sai	131	416	3.18
6.	Kapileswar Bhoi Sai	153	479	3.13
7.	Brahmeswar Patna	72	205	2.85
8.	Kancha Bhoi Sai	77	213	2.77
9.	Laxmi Sagar Bhoi Sai	132	470	3.56
10.	Kapil Prasad Bhoi Sai	128	391	3.05
11.	Matha Bhoi Sai	35	83	2.37
12.	Mangala Sai	25	98	3.92
13.	Ghatikia	200	415	2.08
14.	Shampur	130	509	3.92
15.	Jagamara	50	192	3.84
16.	Baramunda	115	473	4.11
17.	Pokhriput	80	324	4.05
18.	Iginia	117	462	3.73

(Contd...)

(1)	(2)	(3)	(4)	(5)
19.	Siripur Sabar Sai	80	330	4.12
20.	Khandagiri	40	152	3.8
21.	Jadupur	115	500	4.35
22.	Nuagan	172	622	3.62
23.	West Bargarh	85	484	5.69
24.	Nuapal-li Sabar Sai	44	210	4.77
25.	Gobind Prasad	9	79	8.78
26.	Jharapada	58	354	6.10
27.	Chandrasekharpur	38	207	5.45
28.	Tala Ranga Matia	11	64	5.82
29.	Gadakana	87	527	6.06
30.	Patia	132	791	5.99
31.	Gadagopinath Prasad	31	160	5.16
32.	Samari Gadia	28	112	4.0
33.	Palasuni	11	51	4.64
34.	Bhatapada	70	326	4.66
35.	Rasulgarh Sabar Sai	52	168	3.23
36.	Dhoba Sai (old town)	12	61	5.08
37.	Pandra	31	157	5.06
	Sub-total (A)	**2760 (14.45)**	**10,848 (14.67)**	**3.92**
38.	Sikharchandi Nagar	1282	6084	4.75
39.	Dumuduma	1199	5528	4.61
40.	Jokalandi	1761	7678	4.36
	Sub-total (B)	**4242 (22.82)**	**19290 (26.04)**	**4.55**
41.	Kalpana Labour Colony	288	1053	3.66
42.	Budha Nagar	130	505	3.88
43.	Bhima Tangi	30	126	4.2
44.	Vani Vihar (Patharbandha-N)	528	1977	3.74
45.	Vani Vihar (Patharbandha-S)	378	1511	4.0
46.	Vani Vihar Complex	107	346	3.23

(Contd...)

(1)	(2)	(3)	(4)	(5)
47.	Ganda Munda	122	509	4.17
48.	Saheed Nagar Rickshaw Pullers Colony (A)	149	574	3.85
49.	Saheed Nagar Rickshaw Pullers Colony (B)	66	255	3.86
50.	Saheed Nagar Herekrushna Nagar	290	1074	3.70
51.	Saheed Nagar Telenga Sahi	177	671	3.79
52.	Laxmi Sagar Refuge Colony	125	548	4.38
53.	Mancheswar Dhirigut Sahi	185	703	3.8
54.	Mancheswar Patra Sahi	43	201	4.67
55.	Mancheswar Thirigutu Sahi	82	294	3.59
56.	Jagannath Leprosy Colony	52	156	3.0
57.	Savarapalli (Jayadev Vihar)	217	888	4.09
58.	Bayababa Colony (Unit-9)	127	525	4.13
59.	Acharya Vihar (Science Park Basti)	305	1091	3.58
60.	Nuapali Munda Sai	92	369	4.01
61.	Unit-8	271	1201	4.43
62.	Bapuji Nagar	238	931	3.91
63.	Banadurga Colony (Unit 6)	135	532	3.94
64.	Dr. Ambedkar Basti (Unit 6)	77	295	3.83
65.	Unit-6 Sub-station area	118	462	3.92
66.	Unit-6 Sweeper Colony	205	895	4.37
67.	Laxmisagar Basti	321	1116	3.48
68.	Siripur Kandha Sai	43	167	3.88
69.	Delta Paiknager	101	363	3.59
70.	Ganganagar Pali	171	720	4.21
71.	Laxmisagar Haladipadia	116	519	4.47
72.	Nilakantha Nagar	169	539	3.19
73.	Mancheswar Munda Sai	164	622	3.79
74.	Bijunagar (Unit-5)	97	408	4.21
75.	Saheed Nagar Santi Palli	281	1163	4.14
76.	Nolia Sahi and Muslim Basti	124	586	4.73
77.	Bhimpur Bhoi Sai	73	277	3.79
78.	Jharana Sahi	371	1663	4.48

(Contd…)

(1)	(2)	(3)	(4)	(5)
79.	Santi Nagar FCI Colony	143	623	4.36
80.	Ganganagar	70	295	4.21
81.	Unit-3 Labour Colony	100	339	3.39
82.	Unit-3 Hadi Sahi	81	387	4.78
83.	Kedarpalli Nuasahi	131	581	4.44
84.	Budheswari Labour Colony	160	717	4.48
85.	Reddy Basti (old stn sqr)	231	910	3.94
86.	Champua Pokhari	99	365	3.69
87.	Mochi Sahi	118	520	4.41
88.	Budhanagar Sahi	99	395	3.99
89.	Aurobinda Colony	177	760	4.29
90.	Gautam Nagar (Jayadev Vihar)	204	685	3.76
91.	Unit-9 Labour Colony	154	682	4.43
92.	B.J.B. Nagar	277	1130	4.08
93.	Rameswar Patna	107	417	3.9
94.	Samantarapur	141	556	394
95.	Janata Nagar (Jayadev Vihar)	306	912	2.98
96.	Adibasi Sahi (-do-)	582	1614	2.77
97.	Nirankari Nagar (-do-)	373	1256	3.37
98.	Mahabir Nagar (-do-)	294	1050	3.57
99.	Salia Sahi (-do-)	517	1747	3.78
100.	Ekambra Sahi (-do-)	199	419	2.11
101.	Nilachakra Nagar (-do-)	459	1597	3.48
	Sub-total (C)	**11590 (62.34)**	**43792 (59.23)**	**3.78**
	Total (A+B+C)	**18592 (100.00)**	**73930 (100.00)**	**3.97**

Source: Bhubaneswar Municipal Corporation, 1997.

Note: Slums from Sl. No. 1-37 are situated on *Sthitiban* land, from 38-40 are the resettlement colonies, and the rest slums from Sl. No. No. 41-101 are situated on encroached land.

Appendix—3

Average Purchasing and Selling Price (by local godown keepers) of Non-metal and Metal Rag items

Sl. No.	*Items*	*Average price (in Rs.) per kg.* Purchasing price from rag-pickers/ others dealers	Selling price	*Remarks*
(1)	*(2)*	*(3)*	*(4)*	*(5)*
	Non-metal Items			
1.	Boot	9.00	10.50	Leather or those which can be recycled
2.	Broken glass	0.85	1.20	Any broken glass
3.	Carton	2.25	3.50	New or old
4.	Paper	2.25	3.00	Used or unused
5.	Plastic materials	6.58	8.83	
	1st variety	12.25	15.00	Bucket, Jars
	2nd variety	4.00	5.50	Ordinary strings knitting strings etc.
	3rd variety	3.50	5.00	Dairy covers and other such materials
6.	Polythene materials	8.67	11.33	
	1st variety	14.00	18.00	OMFED packs
	2nd variety	8.00	10.00	Dalda and oil packs
	3rd variety	4.00	6.00	Ordinary polythene

(Contd...)

(1)	(2)	(3)	(4)	(5)
	Metal Items			
1.	Aluminium	40.00	50.00	Utensils or others such materials
2.	Brass	70.00	95.00	
3.	Iron	4.00	5.00	
4.	Cast iron	3.00	4.50	
5.	Lid	5.00	7.00	
6.	Tin	2.50	3.50	
	Special Specific Items	0.75	1.20	
1.	Unbroken beer bottle (per piece)	1.25	2.00	
2.	Unbroken medicine bottle (per piece)	0.15	0.40	

Appendix—4

Distribution of street children according to residential places of their parents/guardians

Sl. No.	*Name of Place/Basti/Village*	*Total Cases*	*% age*
(1)	*(2)*	*(3)*	*(4)*
1.	Abandoned/incomplete building	12	10.00
2.	Ainginia Village (Ainginia)	3	2.50
3.	Ashok Nagar (Rajmahal Sqr.)	1	0.83
4.	Coolie Sahi (Budheswari)	7	5.83
5.	FCI Malgodam (Santi Nagar)	20	16.67
6.	Kadali Godam (Budha Nagar)	7	5.83
7.	Kali Basti (Ashok Nagar)	2	1.67
8.	Kolha Sahi (Dumuduma)	4	3.33
9.	Mochi Sahi (Arunjyoti Nagar)	12	10.0
10.	Muslim Sahi (Baramunda)	1	0.83
11.	Pavement (Unit-IV)	1	0.83
12.	Pradhan Basti (Old Station Bazar)	3	2.5
13.	Railway Platform (Master Canteen)	1	0.83
14.	Ragunath Nagar (Baramunda)	4	3.33
15.	Raja Bazar (Khurdha Town)	1	0.83
16.	Salia Sahi (Jajadev Vihar)	12	10.00
17.	Samantarapur Village	1	0.83
18.	Santipali (Saheed Nagar)	10	8.33
19.	Satya Nagar (Aiginia)	6	5.00
20.	Sikhar Chandi (Patia)	12	10.00
	Total	**120**	**100.00**

Appendix—5

Daily minimum wage rate among different categories of labourers

Sl. No.	*Category of worker*	*Minimum wage*
(1)	*(2)*	*(3)*
1.	Unskilled labourer	30.00
2.	Semi-skilled labourer	36.00
3.	Skilled labourer	42.00
4.	Highly skilled labourer	48.00

Note: Basing on the recommendations of minimum wage advisory board, Government of Orissa has adopted to the above minimum wages for different categories of daily workers with effect from 15th August 1996, (cf. Samal, 1996: 113).

Appendix—6

Position of Balashrams run by OSCCW

Sl. No.	*Name of the Balashram*	*Strength of inmates in Balashrams*	*Strength of inmates in destitute homes*	*Total inmates*
(1)	*(2)*	*(3)*	*(4)*	*(5)*
1.	Balasore	60	180	240
2.	Berhampur	50	75	125
3.	Cuttack	40	90	84
4.	Jajpur	40	44	50
5.	Nawarangpur	–	50	50
6.	Puri	–	50	50
	Total	**190**	**489**	**679**

Source: Annual Report of Orissa State Council of Child Welfare, 1996-97, p. 2.

Appendix—7

Achievement of OSCCW under the scheme of rehabilitation of street children and children in difficult circumstances since its commencement

Sl. No.	*Variables*	*Financed by Govt. of India*	*Financed by Govt. of Orissa*	*Total*
(1)	*(2)*	*(3)*	*(4)*	*(5)*
1.	Total No. of centres	6	4	10
2.	No. of children placed back to their families	21	20	41
3.	No. of children provided with education	1250 1	–	1250
4.	No. of children re-admitted in schools	40	17	57
5.	No. of children provided with health services	670	134	804
6.	No. of children placed back in Balashrams	–	3	3
7.	No. of children given facilities of credit for income generation	4		4
8.	No. of children given vocational skills	40	69	109
9.	No. of public and officials who have been oriented on the matter of street children	150	–	150
10.	No. of children provided with shelter facilities	18	–	18

Source: Annual report of Orissa State Council for Child Welfare, 1996-97, p. 4.

Appendix—8

CASE STUDY-1

Zakir Husen is a 14-year-old illiterate Muslim boy. He works as a rag-picker and stays with his parents at FCI Malgodam Basti. His father had migrated from Medinapur district of the State of West Bengal sometime in early 1970s.

He belongs to a family of 9 members. He says that "all our family members are working, still then many times we remain underfed. I have been working as a rag-picker since when I was about 4 years old. I wake up early in the morning; at about 5 A.M. or even earlier and go to work. I come back at about 9.30 A.M. and sells my collection at a rag godown specified by my father. The godown keeper gives me Rs. 4/- as per the instruction of my father for breakfast which I take at a nearby tea shop and again I go for picking rags at about 10.30 A.M. or even immediately after taking breakfast. Now I may work for about 4 hours and come to home for lunch at about 2 P.M. Thereafter, my last phase of work starts at about 3 P.M. and it continues upto 5 or 6 P.M."

At the end of each working day of Zakir, his father collects the cost of his collections at any godown other than the one specified by his father. If he does so or does not give the earned money, he is often scolded, beaten up and at times his food is even denied. His father does not admit him to the house by closing the door. No matter, what Zakir does and what he eats and where he sleeps. His parents feel that this type of discouragement would bring him into the right path.

CASE STUDY–2

N. Ramesh Rao is a 13-year-old *Mochi* (cobbler) boy. He is one of 8 members of his family. He is educated only upto class III and now works as a shoe-shiner at Bhubaneswar railway station.

He says that "my father was a class-IV employee in the railway department. But because of his excessive drinking habit and irregularity in office, he was suspended from his service. Now, he acts as a paid-local goon and is involved in many criminal cases. He has also opened a shoe-repairing shop at aerodrome area but does not work sincerely. He takes advance from many customers, spends it in drinking alcohol and forgets to keep up his word to deliver shoes in time. It creates frustration and anguish in many customers and hence the business of my father is hampered. So, as per the instruction of my father, I often go to his shop, repair the shoes and as far as possible try to satisfy the customers. But few days ago, when my father was absent, a customer from whom my father had taken an advance amount before about fifteen days, came and started throwing out all our belongings from the cabin without any exchange of dialogue with me. When I protested, he beat me up and threatened not to open the shop any more and to shift the cabin to some other place; away from aerodrome area. I was shocked and did not go to that shop any more. But when my father forced me, I developed a conflicting situation with him. He ceased my personal shoe-repairing kit and got me out of home. I stayed with my uncle (father's brother) for some days but I could not meet his demand of huge charge towards my food at his home. I ran off from his home and now, from last 4 days I have been staying at the railway station. At times I sleep on the community-meeting-pendals of our basti. Presently I am managing to work at a road side shoe-repairing shop of my friend. But I am to give three-fourths of the total income to him as the cost of using his instruments and the kit".

He, further says that "if my father dies, it would be a great grace of the God on all of us. I and my mother would be the most happiest persons in that case. Listen sir, one day, just before a month ago, my father asked my elder brother for a large share of his daily income for consuming alcohol. My brother did not yield. But, my father is so cruel that he spread out some kerosene on the body of my brother when he was sleeping and put fire on him. Immediately, I and my mother poured down some buckets of water on the body of my brother and he was saved. In a different case, concerning to his demand of having money from my mother for consumption of alcohol, he stabbed my mother but she was escaped adroitly from being murdered. Now, tell me sir, how can we stay with him? Should not he be murdered by someone else?"

CASE STUDY–3

Laxmi Behra, is a backward caste Hindu girl (cow herder). She has three sisters and one brother. Hence they are 7 members including herself and her parents. She is an illiterate and about 13-year-old.

Laxmi, her parents and other members have come from Nayagarh district sometime in late 1989 with no plan at all as where to stay, what to do and how to earn their daily bread. They had an uncertain future in Bhubaneswar. They reached at the Bhubaneswar railway station, took rest at the platform and since then all of them have been staying over there. Most often railway officials throw their belongings out of the station. They go to a distant place along the railways within the periphery of Bhubaneswar railway platform. After some days, again they come back to take rest under the roof of the platforms. But they are not freed from the same treatment from the railway officials and hence their time is spent in uncertainty, trouble, grief, harassment, ill treatment and torture. Still then within these difficulties, they derive happiness. Her mother says "it is better to live here than going back to village and die over there".

Laxmi is a beggar at the station. She works for the whole day. Her income is mostly saved for her marriage purpose. But as they do not have a closed house in Bhubaneswar, her father goes to his village once after about 3 months to keep their savings with the village sarapanch.

To a question like 'whom do you blame for your present plight', she replies that "we do not have a house either at our village or here in Bhubaneswar. We are very very poor and we do not even get enough rice to cook daily. Most often we remain hungry and hence starve. I do not know who is responsible for this".

CASE STUDY-4

N. Kari is a *Mochi* (cobbler) boy of about 13-year-old. His father was serving as a peon in N.C.C. office, Bhubaneswar. But because of his drunkard nature, he is no more working in that office.

Kari works as a shoe-shiner. With his little uncleaned kit bag containing of shoe-shining materials and shoe-repairing instruments, he appears in front of a number of train-passengers, approaches to get their shoes shined at a very nominal cost and manages to earn about Rs. 25/- a day. Out of his daily income, he was giving about Rs. 10/- regularly to his mother for the smooth management of home and spending about Rs. 8/- to Rs. 10/- for his food independently. He was saving the rest amount with her mother. But his father was always beating his mother and taking away all his savings for consumption of alcohol. So, now he saves about Rs. 5/- daily with his friend Gopi. So far, he has saved about Rs. 200/- and he would buy a woodland shoe when it becomes about Rs. 500/-.

Kari has been a victim to the Municipal Officials for about 4 times last year. For the first two times, they had thrown out his kit while he had opened it at the road side, that tuns from Cuttack road to the railway station and last time they have snatched his shoe repairing instruments, like *Rampi, Jambur,* and *Martul*. But he has not yet gone to the Municipal office to recover the same as he says that the "Municipal officials would ask for a big amount of money as bribe. It would be equal to the cost of my articles ceased by them".

CASE STUDY-5

Ranjan Dakua is a backward caste Hindu school dropout boy from class II. He is about 11-year-old and works on streets to collect potatoes from godown sites at Ainginia, Bhubaneswar. Normally he leaves his bed as early as possible and rushes into the site at about 5 A.M. He takes his hand bag and a sack in it. He works in two phases. The first phase of his work starts from early morning and it continues to about 11 A.M. and the second phase of work covers about 4 hours from 2 P.M. to 6 P.M. During this period he collects about 10 to 15 Kgs. of potato per day depending upon the number of truck-loads reaches at the godown sites. It costs about Rs. 25/- to Rs. 35/- at the rate of Rs. 2.50 per Kg. But he says that when he stays at the godown site for the whole night, he takes a sackful of potato; about 30 kgs. that costs around Rs. 75/- in the market.

Rajnan is enrolled in a non-formal education centre runs at the godown site by Orissa State Council for Child Welfare (OSCCW). It runs from 8 A.M. to 11 A.M. and provides some nutritional incentives to the students at the closing hour every day. But Ranjan is not regular to attend this centre as he is to earn at least 8 to 10 Kgs. of potato daily for his family. Otherwise he is to face some horrible situations at home. However, most often he says that when he feels hungry, he attends the centre and gets some banana or bread or both. In such days he has to work for more hours and returns home very late to take lunch.

CASE STUDY-6

L. Gopinath is a *Mochi* (cobbler) boy, born in Bhubaneswar city after his parents came from Berhampur town in 1982 and settled here. He is educated upto class VIII. He is around 14-year of age.

Gopinath earns his livelihood as a shoe-shiner at Bhubaneswar railway station. He has been practising this job when he was about 7-year-old and was doing class II. His earning comes to Rs. 58/- per day on an average. Of this, he gives about Rs. 20/- to Rs. 25/- daily to his parents for management of home and spends about Rs. 20/- on his food, smoking, gambling and also viewing films. He rotates the rest amount in his petty business. But in the last month he did not give any money to his parents for two consecutive days. It created a serious conflict with his father. His father got Gopinath out of his home. Since then he has been staying at the railway station and sleeping at the railway platform.

He says that he is caught as a suspect in majority of the theft cases at the station and detained at the police station. He cites an unpleasant incidence of his life which he has experienced very recently; about 4 months ago. A purse of a train passenger containing some money was stolen by somebody in a special military coach. But he was immediately caught as a suspect and taken to the police station. He was detained for 3 days. On the fourth day, his family members gave Rs. 200/- to the police and he was released. Fortunately, on the fifth day three thieves were caught in red hand in a pick-pocketing case. One of them, later on, was identified as he who had stolen the purse of that military person in which case Gopinath was a suspect.

CASE STUDY–7

Riaz Khatun is a 12-year-old Muslim girl, engaged in rag-picking. She is the eldest one amongst four children of her parents. She has come from Mohina area of Medinapur district of the state of West Bengal. She is an illiterate.

She ways that "it is good to study at school and get educated but how can I attend school at this age? ----If at all I attend school, then how our home will run? From where money will come for our maintenance?" By this time an elderly Muslim man who was sitting beside me told that "Sir, after some years she will get married. If now she attends school, from where her parents will arrange money for her marriage? Her mother saves the earning of her daughter very tactfully and keeps it for her marriage purpose. Otherwise there would be nothing left as her father takes it for consumption of alcohol".

CASE STUDY–8

Santosh Behera, a school drop-out is about 13-year-old. He has two brothers and one sister. His father died in 1995 but his mother is alive. After the death of his father, he discontinued his study from class IV. Now he works as a vendor and sells boiled egg at railway station. (He is a member of hawkers association consisting of members who subsist on selling of tea, coffee, boiled egg, cucumber, ground-nut, pea, green coconut, bread, traditionally home made cakes and some other edible items, and cold drinks, mineral water etc).

He says that his business is profitable but not free from troubles. Whenever there is a theft case, police catch him as a suspect and detain him in lock at police station. In the current year he has been a prey to the police for two times and he had to give Rs. 100/- each time to be get released. Mrs. Usharani Samal, the local ICDS worker interprets that it is the traditional tactics of the local police to arrest these innocent children as suspects in order to warm up their packets. Once they get some bribe they close the file and release there children. These children fall prey to the police as they are poor and do not have any person who could stand for them.

CASE STUDY-9

S.K. Nazimudin is another Muslim boy. He is about 11-year-old and works as a rag-picker. His father has come from lalbag, Cuttack and is now staying at FCI Malgodam Basti.

He is not studying in class II. Still then he works daily from early morning to about 9 A.M. He sells his collection at a godown adjacent to his basti and takes some tiffin before he goes to school at 10 A.M. He comes back at 5 P.M. On Sundays and holidays he works for the whole day. But in such days he becomes very selfish to spend most of his income on his personal food and in gambling. In that case he is scolded and also beaten up severely. For this, he had ran off from home for twice last month and had spent nights at the local railway station.

CASE STUDY-10

Kuna Behera, aged about 14 years, is an Oriya backward caste Hindu boy. His father had come from Digapahandi area of the district of Ganjam, Orissa, in 1991. He was then studying in class II. But when he came over to Bhubaneswar city, he had to discontinue his study and work for the family. He linked to work as a rag-picker.

Kuna says that like many of his friends, he is quite often suspected by his father of concealing some of his daily income and for this, he is also beaten up. But now he has become an adult and goes to Talcher area for collection of rags. He takes about Rs. 70/- to Rs. 80/- with him and goes to Talcher by train without ticket. He stays over there for about a week either under the open sky or at the railway station and brings his collection to Bhubaneswar for sale. He gets about Rs. 400/- to Rs. 500/- for the collection of a weak or so from Talcher area. However, he has to give Rs. 10/- to the T.T.I. as bribe to bring his collection to Bhubaneswar. He clarifies that while he was working in Bhubaneswar, he had to dispose off all his collections at a specified godown identified by his father and was getting only Rs. 1/- to Rs. 2/- from his parents depending upon their mood. But, now he is absolutely free from this and spends money as per his own wish.

He cooks his own food while on tour to Talcher. But does not give much stress on his personal hygienic condition, like cleaning of teeth and taking bath daily.

One day while picking rags from a colony site at Talcher, some public arrested him suspecting him as if he had stolen an utensil from the courtyard of a resident. He was handed over to the police, but was released after 3 days as he was innocent and not involved in that case.

Bibliography

Adamson, P., 1993, *The Progress of Nations*, New York: Unicef.

—, 1995, *The Progress of Nations*, New York: UNICEF.

—, 1996,, *The State of the World's Children*, New York: UNICEF.

Aphale, C.A., *Growing up in An Urban Complex*. New Delhi: National.

Arbams, Charles, 1964, *Man's Struggle for Shelter in an Urbanizing World*. Cambridge, Mass: The MIT Press.

Archard, D., 1993, *Children: Rights, and Childhood*. London: Routedge.

Arimpoor, Joe, 1992, *Street Children of Madras*, Noida: National Labour Institute.

Basta, S.S., 1977, "Nutrition and Health in Low Income Urban Areas of the Third World", *Ecology of Food and Nutrition*, 6: 113-124.

Black, Maggie, 1991, "Philippines: Children of the Runaway Cities, Case Study in *The Series The Urban Child in Difficult Circumstances*. Flourence: UNICEF/ICDC.

—, 1993, "Street and Working Children", *Report of An Innocent Global Seminar*, Flourence: UNICEF/ICDC.

—, 1996, *Children First*. New York: Oxford University Press.

Blanc, C.S. (ed.), *Children in Distress: Global Predicaments and Innovative Strategies*. Flourence: Gordon and Breach and UNICEF.

—, *Urban Children in Distress: Global Predicaments and Innovative Strategies*, Flourence: UNICEF/ICDC and Gordon and Breach.

BMC, (Bhubaneswar Municipal Corporation), 1995, *Paura Samachar (Oriya)*, Bhubaneswar.

Bose, A., 1971, *Studies in India's Urbanisation 1901-1971*. Bombay: Tata McGraw Hill Publishing Co.

Boyden, Jo and Pat Holden, 1991, *Children of the Cities*, London: Zed Books.

Brown, Lester and Jacobsen, Jodil, 1987, *The Future of Urbanisation: Facing the Ecological and Economic Constraints*, Washington: Worldwatch Institute.

Butterflies, 1994, *My Name is Today, Children News, Vol. II. No. 1*, April-June, New Delhi.

Bwibo, Nimrod O, and Philista P.P. Onyango eds., 1986, *Children in Especially Disadvantaged Circumstances*. UNICEF: University of Nairobi.

Cockburn, T., 1995, *"The Devil in the City: Working Class Children in Manchester 1960-1914"* Paper Delivered are BSA Conference University of Leicester, 11 April, 1995.

CPSW (Council of Professional Social Workers), 1998, CPSW News, Vol. I, No. I, Bhubaneswar.

Cunningham, H., 1991, *The Children of the Poor: Representation of Childhood Science the Seventeenth Century*. Oxford: Blackwell.

D. Lima Hazel and Gosalia, Rima, 1992, *Street Children of Bombay*. Noida: National Labour Institute.

Dingwaney, Manjari et.al, 1988, *Children of Darkness*, New Delhi: Rural Labour Cell.

Denton, John A, 1985, "The Underground Economy and Social Spectrum" *Sociological Spectrum*" 5: 31-42.

Desai, A.R, 1985, *Trends of Urban Development in India and Proliferation of Slums and Squatting*. Bombay: C.G. Shah Memorial Trust Publication.

De Souza, Alfred, 1978, *The Indian City Poverty, Ecology and Urban Development*. New Delhi: Monohar Publications.

Ennew, Judith, 1986, "Children of the Street" *New Internationalist*, October.

—, 1994, *Street and Working Children: A Guide to Planning. London: Save the Children.*

Felsman, J.K., 1985(a), *Street Children: A Selected Bibliography*. Hannover, U.S.A. (ERIC).

—, 1985(b), "Abandoned Children Reconsidered: Preventio, Social Policy and the Trouble with Sympathy", in Proceedings of *International Conference of Prevention, University of Montneal*, April-May.

—, 1986, "Risk and Resiliency in Childhood: The Lives of Street Children" in R. Cole and T.D Ugan. eds. *The Child in Our Times: Resiliency and Vulnerability*, New York: Brunner/ Mazal.

Forum on Street Children and Youth, 1985, *Bibliography* drafted for the Forum on Street Children and Youth, Grand-Bassam, Ivory Coast, 25 February-2 March, 1905.

Franuklined, 1986, *The Rights of Children*, Oxford Blackwell.

Gans, H.J, 1962, *The Urban Villagers*. New York: The Free Press.

Ghosh, A, 1992, *Street Children of Calcutta*, Noida: National Labour Institute.

Giovannoi, J.M, and A. Billingsley, 1970, "Child Neglect Amon the Poor: A Study of Parental Groups", *Child Welfare*, 99: 196-204.

GoI (Govt. of India), 1978, *Report on the Working and Living Conditions of Workers in the Building Construction Industry in Delhi*. Chandigarh: Ministry of Labour, Labour Bureau.

GoO (Govt. of Orissa), 1990, *Orissa State Gazetters*, Orissa, Vol. I, Bhubaneswar, Department of Revenue.

—, 1990-91, *Municipal Statistical Year Book*. Bhubaneswar: Directorate of Economics and Statistics.

—, 1995, *Launching of Orissa State Plan of Action for Children-2000 A.D.*, in September 4, 1995 at Soochana Bhawan by Hon'ble C.M. Sri J.B. Pattnaik, Bhubaneswar.

—, 1995, *Orissa State Plan of Action for Children 2000 A.D.*, Bhubaneswar, Department of Women and Child Development.

—, 1996, *Orissa State Council for Child Welfare (Amendment) Rules*. Bhubaneswar: Department of Women and Child Development.

Grant, J.P., 1994, *The State of the World's Children, New York: UNICEF.*

Heuze Gerand, 1996, *Worker of Another World*, Delhi: Oxford University Press.

Hollnsteiner, Mary Racelis, 1978, "The Deprived World of the Child in Poor Urban Areas," *Assignment Children* 43: 113-114.

Hollnsteiner, M.R and P. Tacon, 1983, "Urban Migration in Developing Countries: Consequences for Families and Their Children" in D.A. Wagner ed. *New Directions for Child Development*, No. 2, San Francisco, Jossey-Bass.

Howland, Patrician L., 1984, *"Emotionally Neglected Children-The Need for an Interaction of Law and Child Psychology" 29 South Dekota Review*, 539.

Hunter, D.R., 1964, *The Slum: Challenge and Response*. New York: The Free Press.

Indian Council for Child Welfare, 1977, *Working Children in Urban Delhi*, New Delhi: ICCW.

Inter-NGO, 1985, "Programme on Street Children and Street Youth," *Bibliography on Street Children*, Geneva.

Jhonson, Band, H.A. Morse, 1968, "Injured Children and Their Parents", *Children*, 15: 147-152.

Jones, G., 1995, *Leaving Home*, Buckingham: Open University Press.

Kaur, Surjit, *Wastage of Children*. New Delhi: Sterling Publishers.

Khan, S., 1997, *Street Children's Research*. Dhaka: Save the Children.

Khandekar, M.A., 1970, *Report on the Situation of Children and Youth in Greater Bombay*, Bombay: TiSS.

Khatu, K.K., et.al, 1983, *Working Children in India* Operations Research Group.

Kitchlu, T.N., 1996, *Exploited Child-A National Problem*. New Delhi: M.D. Publications Pvt. Ltd.

Korr, W.B. Fallon and D. Brielard, 1944, "UN Convention on the Rights of the Child Implications for Social Work Education" *International Social Work*, 37: 333-345.

Langway. L, et.al, 1982, "A Nation of Runaway Kids", *Newsweek*. Vol. 1000, October, 18.

Majumdar, T.K., "The Urban Poor and Social Change: A Study of Squattar Settlements in Delhi: in Alfred de Souza. *The Indian City: Parents Ecology and Urban Development*. New Delhi: Manohar Publication.

Mandal, B.B., 1990, *Child and Action Plan for Development*. New Delhi: Mittal Publications.

Mandal, M.N. (ed.), 1990, *Street Children and Slum Children of India*, Calcutta: Socio Legal Aid Research and Training Centre.

Maniciaux, M, 1984, "Battered, III-Treated, Abandoned", *World Health-The Magazine of the WHO* (January-February).

Maunic, F., 1973, *Disturbed and Troubled Children*, New York: Spectrum Publications inc.

Miljeteig, P., 1997, "The International Effort to Monitor Children's Right" in Ben-Arich and H. Wintersberger eds. *Monitoring and Measuring the State of Children- Beyond Survival*. Eurosocial Report No. 62, Vienna, Austria: European Centre for Social Welfare Policy and Research.

Mishra, Shashi, 1988, *Street Children: A Strategy for an Institutional Plus Programme*. Bombay: Social Welfare Dept., GoI.

Mishra, Sudha, 1988, "*Street Children: A Strategy for an Institutional*-Plus Programmes, Paper Presented in the National Workshop (August 29-30) on Street Children, Organised by National Institute of Social Defence, New Delhi: Ministry of Welfare, Govt. of India.

Mohanty, K.K. and M.R. Acharya, 1990, *Displaced Slum Dwellers of Bhubaneswar and Their Rehabilitation (Project Report)*. Bhubaneswar: Nabakrushna Choudhury Centre for Development Studies, Orissa.

Mohanty, T., 1998, *Orissa Round-up*. Bhubaneswar: TBS.

Mohsin, Nadeem, 1994, *Street Children and Working Children in South Asia'* (Working Paper Prepared for the Independent Commission for Population an Quality of Life, UNESCO) Patna: A.N. Sinha Institute of Social Studies.

Munyakho, Dorothy, 1992, Kenya: Child Newcomers in the Urban Jungle", Case Study in the Series *The Urban Child in Difficult Circumstances*. Innocenti Studies, Flourence: UNICEF/ICDC.

Nagia, Praveen, 1988, *'Impact of Urbanisation on Street Children: A Focus on Delhi'* Paper Presented in the National Workshop (August 29-30) on Street Children, Organised by the National Institute of Social Defence, New Delhi: Ministry of Welfare, Govt. of India.

O' Neill, J., 1994, *The Missing Child in Liberal Theory*. Toronto: University of Toronto Press.

Orissa State Council for Child Welfare and UNICEF, 1994, *Brief Workshop Report on Govt. and NGO Participation for Street and Working Children'*, held on 15-16, 1994 and Organised by OSCCW and UNICEF, Bhubaneswar.

Orissa State Council for Child Welfare, 1997, *Annual Report of OSCCW*, Bhubaneswar.

Pandey, Rajendra, 1991, *Street Children of India*, Allahabad Chugh.

—, 1993, *Street Children of Kanpur*. Noida: National Labour Institute.

Panikar, Rita, 1988, *'Street Children: How do we Reach out them'*, Paper presented in the National Workshop (August 29-30) on Street Children, Organised by the National Institute of Social Defence, New Delhi: Ministry of Welfare, Govt. of India.

—, 1993, 'Status of Children in India' in My Name is Today, Vol. I, No. 2, Butterflies Programme of Street Children and Working Children, New Delhi: Butterflies.

Panikar, Rita and Nagia, Parveen, 1992, *Working an Street Children*. Noida: National Labour Institute.

Penrose, A.E. Evan Smith and M. Thomson, *Kids for Hie: A Child's Right to Protection from Commercial Sexual Exploitation*, London: Save the Children.

Phillips, W.S.K., 1994, *Street Children in India*. New Delhi: Rawat.

Rao, B.V.R. and B. Malick, 1992, *Street Children of Hyderabad: A Situational Analysis*. Noida: National Labour Institute.

Reddy, N., 1992, *Street Children of Bangalore*, Noida: National Labour Institute.

Ruchika Social Service Wing (RSSW), Undated, *Leaflets on Welfare Programmes for Street Children (of RSSW)*, Bhubaneswar: Ruchika Social Service Wing.

Samal, K.C., 1996, *Information Activities Around NALCO (NALCO Nagar and Damanjodi Sector)*, Bhubaneswar: Nabakrusha Choudhury Centre for Development Studies, Orissa.

Sanon, C.G.S., 1998, *Working Children- A Sociological Analysis*. New Delhi: APH Publishing Corporation.

Sengupta, P., 1975, *"Children Work to Live"*, Social Welfare. 23 (1).

Silva, Teressa, 1997, *"Highlights of Situation Studies on Street Children in the Philippines"*, Presented to the Workshop held in Conjunction with the CHILD-HOPE Board, 1987.

Singh, Mausafir et.al., 1979, *Working Children in Bombay—A Study*. New Delhi: NIPCCD (Mimeo).

Smith, N.A. West, and P. Davies, 1994, *Lives of the Young and Homeless*. London: Save the Children.

Souza Alfred, 1979, *Children in India,* Delhi: Manohar.

Stein, Andrew, 1986, "Children of Poverty-Crisis in New York", *New York Times Magazine,* June 8.

Strathdee, R and M. Johnson, 1994, *Out of Care and on the Streets.* London: Centre Point.

Tacon. P., 1983, "Abandoned and Street Children", *Bulletin of the International Association of Podiatry,* 6 (2): 237-241.

Times Communication, 1994, *Bhubaneswar Guide,* Bhubaneswar: TCP.

UNICEF, 1984, "Abandoned and Street Children", *Ideas Forum,* Geneva, No. 18, 3.

—, 1988, *The States of the World's Children.* Oxford University Press.

—, 1987, "Children is Especially Difficult Circumstances", *UNICEF Developmental Education Resource Bulletin,* Geneva, No. 1 (January).

—, 1988, *Situational Analysis of Children in Especially Difficult Circumstances with Focus on Street and Working Children in the Union Territory of Delhi",* A Report Prepared for UNICEF by Praveen Nagia and Rita Panikar Pinto, May, 1988.

—, 1988, *"Background Paper Prepared by the UNICEF", New Delhi, For National Workshop on Street Children held on August 29-30, 1988.* Organised by the Ministry of Welfare, Govt. of India, New Delhi and UNICEF. Regional Office for South Central Asia, New Delhi.

United Nations, 1970, *The Improvement of Slums and Uncontrollable Settlement: Report of the Interregional Seminar on the Improvement of Slums and Uncontrollable Settlements.* Medellin, Colombia, 15 February-1, March, 1970, Department of Economic and Social Affairs, United Nations, New York, ST/TAO/SER/124/1971.

—, 1980, *Patterns of Urban and Rural Population Growth,* Population Studies, No. 68, Dept. of International Economic and Social Affairs, UN, New York, STIESASERA/168/23/ 1980.

—, 1984, *Urbanisation and Components of Urban and City Population Growth*, Population Division of the Dept. of International Economics and Social Affairs, United Nations, Document IESA/P/ICP. 1989/Eg. 11/23-28 February, 1983, Prepared for the International Conference on Population, Mexican City, 1984.

Verhellen, E., 1994, *Convention on the Rights of the Child: Background Motivation Strategies, Main Themes*. Leuven: Garant.

Wadhera, Kiron, 1976, *The New Bread Winners*. New Delhi: Viswa Yuvak Kendra.

Walters, Mark, 1989, "The Homeless Street Children of Latin America", *Readers Digest*. 135 (37-41).

West, A., 1986, *No Fixed Abode. Hull: Humberside Youth Association:* The Warren.

—, 1995, *You are on Your Own: Young Peoples Research on Leaving Care*. London: Save the Children.

Wollons, R. (ed), 1993, *Children at Risk in America. History, Concept and Public Policy*. Albany: State University of New York Press.

Wrenski, J., 1983, "The Poorest of the Poor in the City, Age-old Drive for Human Rights", *Human Rights in Urban Areas*, Paris: UNESCO.

Index